The
Teaching Gap

*Best Ideas from the World's Teachers for
Improving Education in the Classroom*

James W. Stigler
and
James Hiebert

THE FREE PRESS

f**P**

THE FREE PRESS
A Division of Simon & Schuster Inc.
1230 Avenue of the Americas
New York, NY 10020

THE FREE PRESS and colophon are
trademarks of Simon & Schuster Inc.

Designed by MM Design 2000 Inc.

Manufactured in the United States of America

20 19

Library of Congress Cataloging-in-Publication Data

Stigler, James W.
    The teaching gap : best ideas from the world's teachers for improving
education in the classroom / James W. Stigler and James Hiebert
        p.   cm.
    Includes bibliographical references and index.
        1. Mathematics—Study and teaching—United States.
2. Mathematics—Study and teaching—Germany.   3. Mathematics—Study
and teaching—Japan.   4. Comparative education.   I. Hiebert, James.
II. Title.
QA13.S77   1999
510'.71—dc21   99-27270
                                                                CIP

ISBN 0-684-85274-8

This book is

dedicated to the memory of

Albert Shanker

1928–1997

Contents

Preface

T HIS BOOK IS ABOUT teaching and how to improve it. It is not another attempt to bash teachers or blame them for the ills that beset America's schools. It is also not another set of recommendations that tell teachers how to teach. It is, instead, a tribute to the importance of teaching, and to the key role that teachers must play in its improvement. School learning will not improve markedly unless we give teachers the opportunity and the support they need to advance their craft by increasing the effectiveness of the methods they use.

Our viewpoint arises from a collaboration that started more than five years ago. At that time, the Third International Mathematics and Science Study (TIMSS) was well into the planning stages. This study, the latest in a series of international studies stretching back more than thirty years,[1] compared mathematics and science achievement among students in forty-one nations. TIMSS was the most carefully designed international study of achievement ever conducted. One component of TIMSS was a video study that compared the teaching of eighth-grade mathematics in Germany, Japan, and the United States. The video study, on which we collaborated, marked the first time ever that national samples of teachers had been videotaped teaching in their classrooms. For the first time, we could see what teaching actually looks like on a national scale, and we could do this for three countries.

Figuring out how to analyze and summarize these videos was challenging. But it also was a breathtaking experience. We often are blind to the most familiar aspects of our every-day environment, and teaching turns out to be one of these aspects. Looking across cultures is one of the best ways to see beyond the blinders and sharpen our view of ourselves. As we looked again and again at the tapes we collected, we were struck by the homogeneity of teaching methods within each culture, compared with the marked differences in methods across cultures.

Readers who are parents will know that there are differences among American teachers; they might even have fought to move their child from one teacher's class into another teacher's class. Our point is that these differences, which appear so large within our culture, are dwarfed by the gap in general methods of teaching that exist across cultures. We are not talking about a gap in teachers' competence but about a gap in teaching meth-ods. These cross-cultural differences in methods are instructive because they allow us to see ourselves in new ways.

But the teaching gap we describe refers to more than cross-cultural teaching differences. It refers to the difference between the kinds of teaching needed to achieve the educational dreams of the American people and the kind of teaching found in most American schools. Although many of the American teachers we observed were highly competent at implementing American teaching methods, the methods themselves were severely limited.

The teaching gap becomes even more significant when one realizes that while other countries are continually improving their teaching approaches, the United States has no system for improving. The United States is always reforming but not always improving. The most alarming aspect of classroom teaching in the United States is not how we are teaching now but that we have no mechanism for getting better. Without such a mechanism, the teaching gap will continue to grow.

. . .

This book started out as a description of teaching in different cultures based on the data we collected in the video study. As we wrote the book, however, these differences in teaching methods turned out to be only part of the story. Equally important are the general truths we came to understand about teaching and the implications of these truths for the improvement of classroom teaching. Thus, although this book was initially intended as a report of the TIMSS video study, it quickly became much more than that. We do describe mathematics teaching in Germany, Japan, and the United States. But we also examine current reform efforts in the United States, and based on what we learned about teaching and about learning to teach, we propose a new plan for improving classroom teaching in the United States. Because the video study focused on eighth-grade mathematics, most of the classroom examples we present are from eighth-grade mathematics classrooms. The points we make go well beyond mathematics, however—and certainly well beyond eighth grade. Mathematics teachers might find the book especially interesting, but our intention became to write a book that would be of interest to teachers in all subjects at all levels.

Teachers are not the only audience for this book. We have written it for school administrators, policymakers, politicians, and parents. Although teachers hold the key, they teach in a system that currently works against improvement. Unless other important players get involved, our country cannot implement a program that allows teachers to improve teaching. This would be unfortunate, not because it would miss *an* opportunity but because it would miss the *only* opportunity. The system must support teachers to improve teaching, because teachers are the key to closing the gap.

• • •

This book, and the study from which it grew, could not have been completed without the help of many people.

The TIMSS video study was funded by a contract from the National Center for Education Statistics (NCES), U.S. Department of Education, to WESTAT, Inc. The views expressed in this book, however, should in no way be construed to be those of NCES or of the U.S. Department of Education.

We are grateful to Emerson Elliot, past commissioner of NCES, and to Pascal Forgione, the current commissioner, whose support and enthusiasm went well beyond the financial. Lois Peak, the NCES program officer who oversaw the study, worked tirelessly to help us through the intricacies of a government project. Without her unwavering belief in the importance of this work, the study would never have been done. And we thank Nancy Caldwell of WESTAT for her constant and dependable help throughout the contract.

The TIMSS video study could not have been done without the help of our international collaborators. Juergen Baumert and Rainer Lehmann (in Germany) and Toshio Sawada (National Institute of Educational Research, Tokyo) managed the data-collection process and helped us to understand teaching in their countries.

Clea Fernandez, of Teachers College/Columbia University, played a major role in the early planning and conceptualization of the project; Scott Rankin trained the videographers for the study; Takako Kawanaka, Steffen Knoll, and Ana Serrano led our coding-development efforts; Patrick Gonzales managed the transcription and translation process and contributed to our analyses of classroom discourse; Eric Derghezarian, Fumiko Ichioka, and Nicole Kersting worked endless hours in the analysis of videotapes; Gundula Huber and Alyne Delaney handled the digitizing of the tapes; and Ken Mendoza wrote the software that enabled us to manage the huge quantity of video collected in the study. We want to recognize these individuals for the important role they played in the project.

A number of consultants advised us at key points. These included Nicolas Hobar, Christine Keitel, Magdalene Lampert, Gilah Leder, Shin-Ying Lee, Johanna Neubrand, Michael Neubrand, Yukari Okamoto, Hidetada Shimizu, Yoshinori Shimizu, Kenneth Travers, and Diana Wearne. We are grateful for their input.

We could never adequately acknowledge the tireless contribution of our mathematics content group, led by Alfred Manaster. Other members of this group included Phillip Emig, Wallace Etterbeek, and Barbara Wells. Their work greatly enhanced the findings of the study.

The writing of this book was supported in part by a generous grant from the Albert Shanker Institute. We want to express our deep appreciation to the late Albert Shanker for his early support of our efforts, and to Eugenia Kemble and Alice Gill, who followed through on the project after his death.

Many people read drafts of the book at various stages; their suggestions and criticisms have improved the book greatly. These readers include Gail Burrill, Tom Carpenter, Megan Franke, Philip Jackson, Jennifer Jacobs, Jeremy Kilpatrick, Paul Kimmelman, Kevin Miller, Leigh Peake, Sheila Sconiers, Nanette Seago, Lisle Staley, William Stanley, Harold Stevenson, and Karen Stigler. Special thanks go to Ronald Gallimore, our most constant critic, whose good humor, encouragement, insight, and wisdom kept us going. Of course, none of these people are responsible for any flaws in the book (except for maybe Ron).

We also want to thank Susan Arellano, formerly of the Free Press, who believed in the book and sold the idea to the Free Press; and Philip Rappaport, our editor at the Free Press, whose clear vision and timely input helped us write a book that could speak to a real audience.

Finally, we thank our families, whose support and tolerance made this book possible: Karen Stigler, Sam Stigler, Thomas Stigler, and Charlie Stigler; and Diana Wearne.

We welcome your comments on *The Teaching Gap*. Please visit our Web site at www.lessonlab.com/teaching-gap.

CHAPTER 1

The Teaching Gap

C ONDITIONS FOR IMPROVING education in the United States are more favorable today than they have been in a generation. Both politicians and the public recognize that education needs to be improved. Bad news from international comparisons of student achievement is no longer seen as esoteric by the American public; these days it is on the front page and a linchpin of many politicians' stump speeches. In our increasingly global economy, citizens see direct evidence that America's future will depend on the education of its workforce, and they are determined to compete. Education has become a high priority among the electorate.

But the real reason for optimism is that all this attention to education is not just rhetoric. We are witnessing a tidal wave of educational reform that appears to gain momentum with each passing year. Virtually every state in the nation is working to develop high standards for what students should learn in school, along with means for assessing students' progress. In a field where fads have ruled, we are seeing something new: a growing commitment to the idea that clear and shared goals for student learning must provide a foundation on which to improve education and achievement. Without clear goals, we cannot succeed, for we cannot know in which direction to move.

Yet it is equally important to recognize that standards and assessments, though necessary, are not enough. What must be done now is to find ways of providing students with the learning opportunities they need to reach the new standards. Making higher standards a reality for students will require more than just the status quo inside our nation's classrooms; curriculum, assessments, and—above all—teaching must improve dramatically. In our view, teaching is the next frontier in the continuing struggle to improve schools. Standards set the course, and assessments provide the benchmarks, but it is teaching that must be improved to push us along the path to success.

Our contention that standards alone are not enough is shared by many politicians and school reformers, and they stand ready to help. President Clinton has successfully pushed through legislation that will pour millions of dollars into reducing class size in elementary schools nationwide.[1] Many states are actively considering making vouchers and school choice a central part of their educational systems. And many school districts are embarking on additional initiatives, such as creating charter schools, outfitting schools with new technologies, and sanctioning new forms of school management.

We believe that these highly visible efforts, though well intentioned, miss the mark, because they leave out the one ingredient most likely to make a difference in students' learning: the quality of teaching. Reducing the class size from thirty to twenty certainly will make teachers happier. But if teachers continue to use the same methods they used with larger classes, learning opportunities for students will change little. Similarly, implementing a voucher system might increase competition among schools and spur their desire to improve. But desire alone does not provide teachers with the knowledge they need to implement more effective methods. Class size reductions, vouchers, and most other popular efforts to improve schools will end in disappointment if they do not fundamentally improve what happens inside classrooms.[2]

We are not the only ones to decry this lack of attention to the improvement of teaching. Jerome Bruner, an elder statesman in educational psychology, made the same point in his 1996 book, *The Culture of Education:*

It is somewhat surprising and discouraging how little attention has been paid to the intimate nature of teaching and school learning in the debates on education that have raged over the past decade. These debates have been so focused on performance and standards that they have mostly overlooked the means by which teachers and pupils alike go about their business in real-life classrooms—how teachers teach and how pupils learn.[3]

Our goal in writing this book is to convince our readers that improving the quality of teaching must be front and center in efforts to improve students' learning. Teaching is the one process in the educational system that is designed specifically to facilitate students' learning. Of course, there are many other factors that influence learning in a significant way, such as students' home and social life, and the resources of the school and community.[4] We do not want to minimize the importance of these for the well-being of children. But much of what our society expects children to learn, they learn at school, and teaching is the activity most clearly responsible for learning.

Robert Slavin, long a leading educational researcher, made a similar observation in a recent article:

> The problem, I would argue, is that reforms so often debated in the media, in the White House, in Congress, and in statehouses across the country do not touch on the changes needed to fundamentally reform America's schools. . . . These reforms ignore a basic truth. Student achievement cannot change unless America's teachers use markedly more effective instructional methods.[5]

What makes this argument compelling is that not only is teaching essential, it is a process we can do something about. Overemphasizing the importance of nonschool factors that often are, frustratingly, beyond the reach of public policy can become an excuse for not trying to improve. Teaching lies within the control of teachers. It is something we can study and improve.

The Learning Gap and the Need to Improve

Good questions to ask at this point are "Why is it so important to improve teaching?" and "How do we know that improvement is needed? Maybe we are doing fine." Surprising as it may seem, there is considerable controversy about the answers to these questions. Influential educators and writers disagree.[6] One answer is simply that there is always room for improvement; no matter how well our students are doing now, it would be foolish not to try to improve.

The truth, as we see it, however, is that the situation in the United States demands improvement, not just because improvement is possible but because it is needed. Our students *are* being shortchanged. They could be learning much more and much more deeply than they are learning now. In the most recent National Assessment of Educational Progress, a periodic thermometer of students' learning, only 38 percent of America's eighth-graders could figure out a 15 percent tip on the cost of a typical meal, even when given five choices from which they could select the correct answer.[7] Is this good enough?

Beyond the surveys of our own country's students, there are a number of sobering international reports. Several years ago, one of us coauthored a book called *The Learning Gap*.[8] That book presented a study of schooling and achievement in Japan, Taiwan, China, and the United States. The findings were cause for concern: As early as fifth grade, U.S. students lagged far behind their counterparts in the other countries. On a test of mathematics achievement, for example, the highest-scoring classroom in the U.S. sample did not perform as well as the lowest-scoring classroom in the Japanese sample.

Interest in international studies has grown since publication of *The Learning Gap*, heightened recently by release of the results of the Third International Mathematics and Science Study (TIMSS). As the name implies, this was the third in a series of international studies. The first was conducted in the 1960s and the second in the early 1980s. In both of these studies, U.S. students performed quite poorly compared with their peers in most Asian and many European countries.[9] But neither of these two earlier studies came close to matching the size and quality of the TIMSS, by far the most comprehensive and methodologically sophisticated cross-national comparison of achievement ever completed. TIMSS investigated mathematics and science achievement among fourth-, eighth-, and twelfth-grade students in forty-one nations.[10]

The results from TIMSS have garnered a great deal of media interest and have caught the attention of politicians, policymakers, and the general public. The results are dramatic, and they do not paint a flattering picture of American education. For example, in eighth-grade mathematics, twenty of the forty-one nations scored significantly higher, on average, than the United States, while only seven nations scored significantly lower than the United States. The seven nations scoring lower than the United States were Lithuania, Cyprus, Portugal, Iran, Kuwait, Colombia, and South Africa. Nations scoring significantly higher than the United States included Singapore, Korea, Japan, Canada, France, Australia, Hungary, and Ireland.

Of course, the results of large international studies are always open to question. So much differs across cultures and educational systems, it is hard to know where to find the most meaningful comparisons. Are the samples comparable? Do we even have the same goals for education across cultures? Although the answers to these questions are important for interpreting the differences, the gap in achievement between U.S. students and those in other countries is simply too wide to be dismissed on methodological grounds. U.S. education is in need of improvement.

Beyond the Learning Gap

Americans increasingly are aware of this learning gap and are seeking ways to address it. The international comparisons grab the front-page headlines, and officials try to infer recommendations from how one country performs compared with the performance of another. Policymakers carefully study, state by state, scores on the most recent National Assessment of Educational Progress, as if one could divine a strategy, from the scores, for improving performance. Scores of all local schools are printed in the newspaper, and school boards and parents discuss why students in some schools score much lower than others.

As important as it is to know how well students are learning, examinations of achievement scores alone can never reveal how the scores might be improved. We also need information on the classroom processes—on teaching—that are contributing to the scores. Unfortunately, many policymakers have ignored this fact, making decisions about the future of education without even the most rudimentary information about what is happening in classrooms. In 1995, faced with low reading and mathematics performance on the National Assessment of Educational Progress, California's superintendent of public instruction formed two task forces, one for mathematics and one for reading, to study the situation and propose solutions. California, after all, was highly respected for its Curriculum Frameworks that guide reading and mathematics instruction in the state.[11] The Frameworks provided a comprehensive outline for what students should learn and guidelines for appropriate instructional methods. If the Frameworks were so good, why was achievement so low?

In meetings of California's mathematics task force, the discussion often turned to the Frameworks. Were the teaching methods or curricular emphases recommended in the Mathematics Framework perhaps to blame for students' low achievement? A debate ensued among members of the task force, a debate that has been reflected more broadly in public debate around the country between proponents of "reform" teaching and those in favor of more "traditional" teaching methods.[12] Some believed that the Frameworks were not working and should be changed; others believed that the state should stay the course. But often lost in the discussion was a key fact: the state of California had collected no data on the extent to which the Frameworks had been *implemented* in the state's classrooms. This did not stop the state, however, from undertaking a revision of its Mathematics Framework. But on what basis could the Framework be revised? Without knowing what teachers were doing, how could the effectiveness of the Framework be determined?

We do not mean to single out California; no state that we know of regularly collects and uses data directly related to instructional processes in the classroom. Policymakers adopt a program, then wait to see if student achievement scores will rise. If scores do not go up—and this is most often what happens, especially in the short run—they begin hearing complaints that the policy isn't working. Momentum builds, experts meet, and soon there is a new recommendation, then a change of course, often in the opposite direction. Significantly, this whole process goes on without ever collecting data on whether or not the original program was even implemented in classrooms—or, if implemented, how effective it was in promoting student learning. If we wish to make wise decisions, we need to know what is going on in typical classrooms.

Fortunately, the same TIMSS that generated a new wave of concern about students' achievement also collected a wealth of information about educational factors that might help us understand the different levels of performance in different countries. TIMSS researchers analyzed textbooks; asked administrators, teachers, and students about their beliefs and practices; and videotaped teachers teaching typical lessons. The TIMSS video study of teaching, which forms the basis for this book, is especially significant because it provides a penetrating and unparalleled look into classrooms in three different countries. For the first time, we had a full video record of a representative sample of U.S. classrooms. More than that, we had the same kind of information from Germany and Japan. We could now compare more than achievement scores. We could examine similarities and differences in the instructional methods that lay behind these scores.

A Unique Opportunity

The data collected in the TIMSS video study allow us to answer questions that we could not answer previously yet are crucial for the formation of education policy in the years to come. What are the instructional methods that most teachers currently use? Are the highly publicized reform recommendations being implemented in the classrooms of the United States? Are there alternative ways of teaching in other cultures, or is mathematics teaching pretty much the same everywhere? As was pointed out earlier, a major obstacle in our efforts to improve education is the dearth of information about what is happening in our nation's classrooms. Video provides us with a unique way of gathering the information we need to examine our current practices and then improve them.

Video data, such as that collected in TIMSS, also help us discover new ideas about teaching. If alternative ways of teaching exist, video will capture them, even when they lie completely outside our society's current theories of teaching and learning. And because the new ideas are illustrated through actual classroom teaching, they can have immediate practical significance for teachers. Video information can shake up the way we think and let us take a fresh look at classrooms.

What We Have Learned
from the Video Study

As we look back over what we have learned from the TIMSS video study, several things stand out. We foreshadow these things here because they form the basis for the book you are reading.

Teaching, Not Teachers, Is the Critical Factor

Americans focus on the competence of teachers. They decry the quality of applicants for teaching positions and criticize the talent of the current teaching corps. But we come away with a different conclusion: Although variability in competence is certainly visible in the videos we collected, such differences are dwarfed by the differences in *teaching methods* that we see across cultures. (In Chapters 2, 3, and 4 we present our analyses of teaching and describe what teaching looks like in each country.)

We have watched many examples of good teachers employing limited methods that, no matter how competently they are executed, could not lead to high levels of student achievement. Although there are teachers using extraordinary methods in all cultures, the extraordinary is not what defines most students' classroom experiences. Students' day-to-day experiences are mainly determined by the methods most commonly used by teachers within a culture. Cross-cultural differences in these commonly used methods are what we have termed the "teaching gap."

What we can see clearly is that American mathematics teaching is extremely limited, focused for the most part on a very narrow band of procedural skills. Whether students are in rows working individually or sitting in groups, whether they have access to the latest technology or are working only with paper and pencil, they spend most of their time acquiring isolated skills through repeated practice. Japanese teaching is distinguished not so much by the competence of the teachers as by the images it provides of what it can look like to teach mathematics in a deeper way, teaching for conceptual understanding. Students in Japanese classrooms spend as much time solving challenging problems and discussing mathematical concepts as they do practicing skills.

Teaching Is a Cultural Activity

To put it simply, we were amazed at how much teaching varied across cultures and how little it varied within cultures. When we started, we believed there would be great variability in teaching methods within the United States. Political battles between advocates of, among other teaching techniques, phonics and whole language, and basic skills and conceptual understanding, would lead most Americans to assume that there are many different paths that teachers can follow. But these differences paled when we looked across countries from a cross-cultural, comparative perspective. Although we saw variation in the U.S. videos we collected, comparing them with videos from Germany and Japan allowed us to see something we could not see before: a distinctly American way of teaching, which differs markedly from the German way and from the Japanese way.

Teaching is a cultural activity. We learn how to teach indirectly, through years of participation in classroom life, and we are largely unaware of some of the most widespread attributes of teaching in our own culture. (In Chapters 5 and 6 we pull together what we have learned about teaching and argue that if we are going to improve teaching, we must appreciate its cultural character.) The fact that teaching is a cultural activity explains why teaching has been so resistant to change. But recognizing the cultural nature of teaching gives us new insights into what we need to do if we wish to improve it.

A Gap in Methods for Improving Teaching

Finally, we have learned a great deal from the video study about the results of efforts to improve teaching in the United States. Earlier in this chapter we pointed to the dearth of information about the effects that educational policies have in the classroom. The videos provide us with this kind of information, and it is quite striking. Although most U.S. teachers report trying to improve their teaching with current reform recommendations in mind, the videos show little evidence that change is occurring. Furthermore, when teachers do change their practice, it is often in only superficial ways.

This will not surprise those who have worked in the field of teacher professional development. The problem of how to improve teaching on a wide scale is one that has been seriously underestimated by policymakers, reformers, and the public in this country. The American approach has been to write and distribute reform documents and ask teachers to implement the recommendations contained in such documents. Those who have worked on this problem understand that this approach simply does not work. The teaching profession does not have enough knowledge about what constitutes effective teaching, and teachers don't have a means of successfully sharing such knowledge with one another.

To really improve teaching we must invest far more than we do now in generating and sharing knowledge about teaching. This is another sort of teaching gap. Compared with other countries, the United States clearly lacks a system for developing professional knowledge and for giving teachers the opportunity to learn about teaching. American teachers, compared with those in Japan, for example, have no means of contributing to the gradual improvement of teaching methods or of improving their own skills. American teachers are left alone, an action sometimes justified on grounds of freedom, independence, and professionalism. This is not good enough if we want excellent schools in the next century. (In Chapters 7, 8, and 9 we discuss the problem of how to improve teaching, and offer a proposal to make improving teaching the focus of our efforts to close the achievement gap.)

We opened this chapter by describing the opportunities that exist at present for improving education. In this positive environment, the challenge that awaits our nation is to find a way to improve classroom teaching so that our educational goals can be realized.

CHAPTER 2

Methods for Studying Teaching in Germany, Japan, and the United States

T HE STORY OF the TIMSS video study begins in 1993, when, for the first time in history, plans were made to videotape an international sample of eighth-grade mathematics teachers. Each teacher would be videotaped teaching one lesson in his or her own classroom.

Imagine a videographer, Ron Kelly, traveling around the United States for seven months, loaded with equipment, taping in a different school each day. At the same time, Andrea Lindenthal was driving around her native Germany, filming a different mathematics lesson each day, and Tadayuki Miyashiro was doing the same thing in Japan. They all were collecting data for the Third International Mathematics and Science Study.

Birth of the TIMSS Video Study

Planning for TIMSS was largely funded by the U.S. government, through the National Center for Education Statistics and the National Science Foundation. Long before any data were collected, teams of researchers were meeting and designing the tests and questionnaires that would be administered in forty-one countries.[1] Most officials anticipated that American students would not fare well in the cross-national comparisons. The previous international comparisons had provided ample warning. But many of those involved in planning this study now understood that just worrying about low achievement scores would not help improve the scores. This time, officials wanted to be ready to discuss the reasons for low levels of student achievement and to suggest ways to improve achievement. They consulted widely with experts in mathematics and science education, looking for new ways of studying the processes that lead to student learning.

From early on, there was a great deal of interest in collecting information on classroom instruction. Yet there was little agreement on how to do this. Previous large-scale international work had relied on questionnaires to collect information, a relatively inexpensive procedure. Perhaps teachers could be sent a questionnaire and asked to describe the methods they used. The problem was that it would be hard to interpret their responses. It is difficult to know how accurately teachers describe their methods and what they mean by the words they use. For example, if a teacher says she does "problem solving" (currently a popular phrase) with her students, what, exactly, does she do? Different teachers use the same words to mean different things.

Videotaping teachers teaching in their own classrooms

would solve this problem, but it was a radical idea. Video has been around for some time, and researchers have used it to study teaching. But no one had used video to collect a national sample of anything, certainly not teaching. The logistical problems alone were daunting. But the opportunity to peer into the classrooms of various countries was too exciting to pass up.

So was born the video study. Because the goal was to find out more about some of the things that might account for students' performance, the planners wanted to videotape teaching in a variety of countries. But which ones? Videotaping in all forty-one countries was impossible, for both logistical and financial reasons. Three countries were chosen: the United States, Japan, and Germany. Japan was an obvious choice because it has always scored near the top in international comparisons of mathematics achievement. Germany, though it had not participated previously in the large international studies, was also considered an important comparison country, because Germany, like Japan, is a major economic competitor of the United States. The stage was set.

Goals of the TIMSS Video Study

Although the challenges of using video on a large scale are considerable, the major goals of the TIMSS video study were simple and straightforward:

1. To learn how eighth-grade mathematics is taught in the United States.
2. To learn how eighth-grade mathematics is taught in two comparison countries, Germany and Japan.

3. To learn something about the way American teachers view reform and whether they are implementing teaching reforms in their classrooms.

These goals point us toward the first step we must take to improve education in the United States. They focus attention on classroom teaching and on collecting basic information on the instructional methods we currently are using. They allow us to answer fundamental questions that until now we could only guess at: "How do most American teachers teach?" and "How does this compare with how their peers in other countries teach?"

Research Methods: The Nuts and Bolts

We started this chapter with three videographers, one in each country, traveling from school to school. Let us go back to describe in more detail how the video study was conducted.[2]

Once inside the classroom, the videographers collected two main types of data: a videotape of the lesson and a questionnaire response from the teacher. They also collected supplementary materials, such as copies of textbook pages or worksheets, that were helpful for understanding the lesson. Each classroom was videotaped for one complete lesson on a date convenient for the teacher.

Because there are a number of ways in which the integrity of a study like this could be undermined, it is important to understand a few key features of the study. Having confidence in the findings depends on knowing how we dealt with the following issues.

Which Classrooms Should Be Videotaped?

The sample of the study is crucial: If we were to produce a national-level portrait of eighth-grade mathematics instruction, we needed to be sure that the sample of teachers was representative of eighth-grade mathematics teachers. Fortunately, the TIMSS sampling plan was highly sophisticated, and the video sample was constructed to be a random subsample of the full TIMSS sample.

Selecting classroom lessons was not easy. Schools were selected first, then teachers, and then classes. Often we were asked by the school to substitute one teacher for another, or by the teacher to videotape a different class period than the one that had been sampled. We allowed no substitutions of either sort, because to do so would have introduced bias into the study.

The final sample was a "national probability sample." This technical term means that every eighth-grade math teacher in the country and each of the teacher's classes had an equal chance of being selected for the study. This was true in all three of the countries studied. The final video study sample included 231 eighth-grade mathematics classrooms: 100 in Germany, 50 in Japan, and 81 in the United States.[3] Although the number of lessons was not large, because they were sampled randomly we could be sure that they approximated, in their totality, the mathematics instruction to which students in the three countries were exposed. In short, we had a sample that met the highest standards in statistical methodology.

Will the Camera Change What the Teacher Does?

Many people wonder whether the videotapes show what teachers normally do when the camera is not present. Teachers knew, after all, that the videographer was coming. Surely they would try to prepare in some way. They might even go so far as to design a special lesson just for the videotaping. Even if this did not happen, the presence of the camera might affect a teacher's behavior in subtle, unconscious ways. This was a serious concern, and we did not take it lightly.

We explained the goal of the study to all the teachers and asked them to teach the same lesson they would have taught if the camera had not been there. Most teachers do not want to bias a research study, but some might inadvertently do so to please or impress the researchers. We told them we wanted to see a typical lesson, the one they had originally scheduled for that day.

To check on typicality, we asked teachers to describe in the questionnaire what they did in the same class the previous day and what they were planning to do the next day. This helped us to determine whether the teacher had taught a special, stand-alone lesson for the camera or whether, as we hoped, the taped lesson fit within an ongoing sequence. Teachers' responses indicate that few lessons were stand-alone, and we believe most were quite typical.

Finally, we used common sense in deciding the kinds of indicators that might be susceptible to bias and took this into account when interpreting the results. It seems likely, for example, that students were on their best behavior in front of the camera, so we believe the videotapes do not show the normal frequency with which teachers must discipline students. On the other hand, it seems unlikely that teachers asked completely different kinds of questions while being videotaped than they did when the camera was not present. Some behaviors, such as the routines of classroom discourse, are so highly socialized that they are almost automatic and are difficult to change.

Turning Videos into Information

After we collected the videos, the difficult task of analysis began. Meaning is not contained in the videos; it must be constructed by the researcher through a difficult and painstaking process. We began this process in May 1994 with a set of nine trial tapes from each country. A team of six code developers— two from Germany, two from Japan, and two from the United States—and several mathematics educators spent the summer at UCLA watching and discussing the contents of the tapes. Our goal was to understand how teachers construct and implement lessons in each country, and to develop a common language for describing the lessons.

The process was a straightforward one: we would watch a tape (subtitled in English), discuss it, and then watch another. Anyone could stop the tape at any time. The discussion was so vigorous that it often would take a day or more to get through a single lesson. There were disagreements in the group about the contents of the tapes, and especially about how to describe them. But gradually, as we worked our way through the twenty-seven tapes, we began to develop a common view of the nature of teaching in the three countries. More than that, we began to develop a coding system to compare teaching across the three countries.

Many people who are unfamiliar with behavioral research do not understand how it is possible to code video objectively. They assume that there is only one thing to do with video: watch it. But there is a great deal more one can do. It is possible to move beyond individual impressions and identify features of the events portrayed in a video objectively, so that anyone who watches can agree. These objective judgments can be used to quantify the events on the video so that one can know how frequently different categories of activities occur.

The process begins with a discovery that is turned into a hypothesis. For example, we might notice that German teachers develop concepts more fully than do U.S. teachers, or that Japanese teachers ask more open-ended questions than do German and U.S. teachers. We then propose this "discovery" as a hypothesis. The next step is to write a definition that will communicate to other coders what "counts as" developing a concept or as asking an open-ended question. Anyone who has engaged in this process knows that it is not easy to write such a definition. But it can be done. For example, how do you even know something is a question? Would something like "Do you think you could open the door?" count as a question just because it ends with a question mark? Clearly it should not, because in American culture such a statement is a request, not a question.

The test of how successful we were in developing objective codes was the degree to which independent coders made the same judgment when viewing the same segment of video. The convention in behavioral research is to accept as reliable only those codes on which independent coders make the same decision at least 80 percent of the time. All the codes we discuss in this book met this criterion.

The process of turning videos into information yielded two kinds of products: impressions or images of teaching in each country, and quantified results that indicate how often specific features of teaching occur in each country. The images are vivid and powerful. One picture, it is said, is worth a thousand words; one video may be worth millions. On the other hand, the images produced by video can be too powerful, because they can focus attention on one striking example, even when the example is not typical. Coded data help correct these errors and may themselves lead to interesting discoveries. So both kinds of information are crucial for learning about teaching across cultures.

We now turn to the results of the study, and we begin with the first kind of information—images of teaching in Germany, Japan, and the United States.

CHAPTER 3

Images of Teaching

I N THE FALL of 1994, after several months of watching tapes, the project staff met to present some preliminary impressions and interpretations. We invited distinguished researchers and educators from Germany, Japan, and the United States to attend, and we listened intently to what they had to say. We were ready for a fresh perspective. It came late on the last day of the meeting. One of the participants, a professor of mathematics education, had been relatively silent throughout the day. We asked him if he had any observations he would like to share.

"Actually," he began, "I believe I can summarize the main differences among the teaching styles of the three countries." Everyone perked up at this, and here is what he had to say: "In Japanese lessons, there is the mathematics on one hand, and the students on the other. The students engage with the mathematics, and the teacher mediates the relationship between the two. In Germany, there is the mathematics as well, but the teacher owns the mathematics and parcels it out to students as he sees fit, giving facts and explanations at just the right time. In U.S. lessons, there are the students and there is the teacher.

I have trouble finding the mathematics; I just see interactions between students and teachers."

Many of those present were somewhat dumbfounded by this description. How grossly oversimplified it seemed! It also was harshly critical of the American style of teaching and was disturbing to hear. But the image stayed with us, and as we watched the tapes over and over we began to understand that our colleague had captured an important aspect of what we saw in the tapes from all three countries. Although perhaps over-simplified, our colleague's description helped us to see features that might otherwise have been hidden within the noise and complexity of classroom life. Simplified descriptions provide an important starting point for understanding complex activities, provided we are open to revising, tempering, or even discarding them when they outlive their usefulness.

We begin our journey into the TIMSS videos with our own simplified descriptions of teaching in each country. We then present a typical lesson from each country. Because we realize that the typical lesson could never describe every teacher, we conclude the chapter by reporting some ways in which lessons might vary from the typical. Our goal is to help create accurate and rich visual images of teaching in each country.

Preliminary Descriptions of Teaching

Our impression is that teachers in Germany are in charge of the mathematics and that the mathematics is quite advanced, at least procedurally. In many lessons, teachers lead students through a development of procedures for solving general classes of problems. There is concern for technique, where technique includes both the rationale that underlies the procedure and the precision with which the procedure is executed. A good motto for German teaching would be "developing advanced procedures."

In Japan, teachers appear to take a less active role, allowing their students to invent their own procedures for solving problems. And these problems are quite demanding, both procedurally and conceptually. Teachers, however, carefully design and orchestrate lessons so that students are likely to use procedures that have been developed recently in class. An appropriate motto for Japanese teaching would be "structured problem solving."

In the United States, content is not totally absent, as was portrayed by our colleague, but the level *is* less advanced and requires much less mathematical reasoning than in the other two countries. Teachers present definitions of terms and demonstrate procedures for solving specific problems. Students are then asked to memorize the definitions and practice the procedures. In the United States, the motto is "learning terms and practicing procedures."

What do the mottoes "developing advanced procedures," "structured problem solving," and "learning terms and practicing procedures" look like in actual classrooms? In the following sections we describe three actual lessons selected to typify the lessons sampled from each country.

Portraits of Eighth-Grade Mathematics Lessons

The Classrooms

Even though the videotaped classrooms are located thousands of miles apart and in different cultures, they look much the same.

Rows of students' desks, posters on the walls, the teacher's desk and a chalkboard in front—all provide few clues about the country from which the video comes. Students filing into class, individually and in pairs, jostling and joking and laughing, create a remarkably similar atmosphere in each country.

But there are differences. Although German and American students often dress alike—casually, in denim pants and T-shirts or sweatshirts—Japanese students usually dress in school uniforms: special jackets for boys, blouses and skirts for girls. There are fewer students in the German and U.S. classrooms than in the Japanese classrooms. The national average for eighth-grade class size in each country is twenty-five in Germany and the United States, and thirty-seven in Japan.

The typical lessons we describe in this chapter are from classrooms found in somewhat different school situations. In Germany, eighth-graders attend different schools based on their academic achievements and aspirations. The classroom we describe is located in a *Realschule,* the middle track of the three-tiered German school system. Most students attending a *Realschule* will not go on to university, but many expect to enroll in a technical or vocational college. The classroom in Japan is located in a small-city public school with no special distinctions. Japan has no system for tracking students in elementary and middle school. All eighth-graders take the same mathematics course, so the classroom we describe contains students of mixed achievement levels. The classroom in the United States is located in a large public school in the suburbs of a sprawling metropolitan area. The school offers only one mathematics course in eighth grade, so, as in Japan, the classroom contains students of mixed achievement levels.

What about the lessons themselves? Again, there are some interesting similarities and some striking differences. The lessons we describe are about the same length, forty-five to fifty minutes. Some of the time in each lesson is devoted to teacher presentation, some to class discussion, and some to student work. But if the mottoes suggested earlier mean anything, there must be some significant differences in what happens during these activities and how they are arranged. To really understand the differences in classroom teaching, one needs to look carefully at the details of typical lessons, because this is where the teaching gap is revealed. The teaching gap is not an abstract idea concocted by ivory tower researchers; the teaching gap is a set of real differences in the teaching methods used every day in typical classrooms. These differences that accumulate over time and across the country are bound to affect what and how students learn.

Studying the details of lesson design is important but not always easy. The following table might be helpful because it gives an overview of the three lessons we describe and it includes our observations about what features of the lessons typify teaching in each country. To appreciate the sometimes subtle but profound differences in teaching, however, one must study the lessons themselves.

A German Lesson: Developing Advanced Procedures

When the bell rings, Mr. Eisner, the teacher, greets the students: "Good morning."[1] The students respond, "Good morning," and Mr. Eisner says, "Okay, let's start right away, as usual, with our homework." As students pull out their worksheets, Mr. Eisner checks attendance by glancing around the room and recording the students who are absent.

TIME	GERMAN LESSON	JAPANESE LESSON
1 min	Teacher checks homework by calling on students for answers. Students work more difficult homework problems on board. Teacher corrects terminology. *Note: Typical for teacher to be careful about notation and language. Unusual to spend this much time checking homework.*	Teacher reviews yesterday's lesson and assigns a problem that was not finished.
		Students present solution methods they have found, and teacher summarizes.
10 min		Teacher presents task for the day and asks students to work on it independently (task is to invent problem for classmates to solve). *Note: Typical to present task for the day and allow students to solve it in their own way. Often, task can be solved using method students have learned recently.*
20 min	Teacher presents problem for the day—a theorem for students to prove—and leads them through the proof. Teacher emphasizes the procedures that can be used to prove theorems like this. *Note: Proving a theorem is unusual, but the teacher leading the students through a discussion of advanced procedures is common.*	
		Teacher suggests they continue their work in small groups. Leaders of groups share problems with teacher, who writes them on board. Students copy problems and begin working on them.
30 min	*Often, a student will be at the board for part of the discussion.*	*Note: Unusual for students to work this long without a class discussion. Typical for students to struggle with task before teacher intervenes.*
	Class reviews the theorem by students reading aloud from a handout.	
40 min		
	Teacher assigns homework. *Note: Typical to allow no class time for working on homework.*	Teacher highlights a good method for solving these problems. *Note: No homework is typical.*

U.S. LESSON	AUTHORS' NOTES

<table>
<tr><td>

Teacher asks students short-answer review questions.
Note: Typical to begin with "warm-up" activity.

</td><td>

Opening
Common for lessons in all countries to begin with review. But Germany and the United States begin with relatively long segments of checking homework; Japan begins with a quick review of yesterday's lesson.

</td></tr>
<tr><td>

Teacher checks homework by calling on students for answers.
Note: A common way to check homework.

</td><td>

Heart of the Lesson
Germany: Teacher leading students through the development of advanced techniques for solving challenging problems, with students responding to frequent questions.

</td></tr>
<tr><td>

Teacher distributes worksheet with similar problems. Students work independently.

</td><td>

Japan: Students working on challenging problem and then sharing their results.
United States: Teacher engages in

</td></tr>
<tr><td>

Teacher monitors students' work, notices some confusion on particular problems, and demonstrates how to solve these.
Note: Typical for teacher to intervene at first sign of confusion or struggle.

</td><td>

quick-paced question/answer with students, demonstrates methods, and asks students to work many similar problems.

</td></tr>
<tr><td>

Teacher reviews another worksheet and demonstrates a method for solving the most challenging problem.

</td><td>

Closing
The lessons conclude in different ways: Germany and the United States often with assigning homework; Japan with the teacher summarizing the main point(s) of the lesson.

</td></tr>
</table>

Teacher conducts a quick oral review of problems like those worked earlier.

Teacher asks students to finish worksheets.
Note: Unusual to not assign homework.

Checking Homework. Mr. Eisner then calls on students, one at a time, to give the answer to the next problem on the worksheet. After each response, he looks up to see if anyone disagrees. If so, he asks for other responses and endorses one of these as correct, or explains why the error might have been made and gives the correct answer. The first eleven problems are quite straightforward. They require finding the measure of the third angle in a triangle, given the first two, as in the drawing below. Students must simply add the measures of the two angles and subtract from 180 to find the measure of the missing angle.

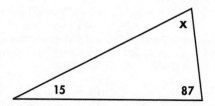

But the next problems are more challenging. One presents the drawing below and asks students to find the angles labeled with capital letters. Students apparently had more trouble with these at home, and there is disagreement about the answers.

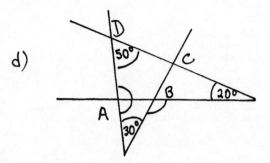

Mr. Eisner asks a volunteer to come to the board to explain the solution. As the student works, Mr. Eisner corrects errors, elaborates on the descriptions provided by the students, and makes sure students are using correct mathematical language. The discussion regarding the problem shown above begins as follows.

Mr. Eisner: Which one could we figure out with the help of the indicated measures? Birgit? It's best if you come to the front, because it's always a little difficult describing it having so many angles.

Birgit: This is one hundred ten degrees (*pointing to the angle opposite A*).

Mr. Eisner: You claim one hundred ten degrees. Can you add an explanation to that?

Birgit: Yes. Because it's in the triangle of fifty degrees and twenty degrees.

Mr. Eisner: Yes, I'll show it again. You are talking now about this triangle (*pointing to the large triangle*). That's twenty degrees and that's fifty degrees, and therefore this third angle has to be, inevitably?

Birgit: One hundred ten degrees.

The rest of this problem, and the remaining homework problems (twenty-two in all), are checked in a similar way. It is now fourteen minutes into the lesson.

Presenting the Topic for the Day. Mr. Eisner presents the new problem that will define today's lesson.

Mr. Eisner: Questions, disagreements concerning homework? Good, then we will construct a little. We need our

tools for that. Okay, please draw first an arbitrary
distance AB. I wouldn't make it too small, but
there has to be space above the distance so we
can put a semicircle there. . . . Okay, construct
now for the distance AB the perpendicular line at
the midpoint. . . . Actually, I don't care so much
about the perpendicular line but only about the
midpoint. . . . Around M [the midpoint] we will
now draw a semicircle.

After the construction, which takes about five minutes, Mr.
Eisner asks the students to "mark on the edge of the circle five
arbitrary points and call them C_1, C_2, . . . C_5" and then "connect with point A and point B so five triangles emerge." A
sample drawing now looks like this:

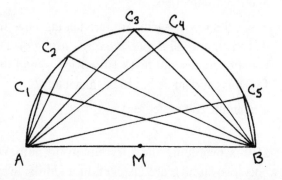

Mr. Eisner asks the students to measure, with their protrac-
tors, all five angles at the five C's. After a few minutes, the
students begin reporting that all five angles are the same size;
they all measure 90 degrees. Mr. Eisner pretends to be startled
by this result and tries to get students to share his surprise. He
then notes that an ancient Greek mathematician (Thales)
found that all angles drawn inside a semicircle like this will

measure 90 degrees. Now the stage is set, and Mr. Eisner presents the real challenge: "We did check it, but we also want to prove it, of course. . . . Prove that it really has to be that way and can't be any other way."

Here we see the advanced nature of the mathematics in German classrooms: proving the Law of Thales is a challenging task for eighth-graders.

Working Through the Proof. As is common in Germany following the presentation of a challenging problem, Mr. Eisner neither leaves the students alone to complete the task by themselves nor demonstrates a quick method that students are supposed to imitate. Using the drawing below, he leads the class through a careful development of the proof.

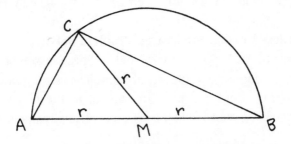

Two triangles, AMC and BMC, have radii for two of their sides, so they are isosceles triangles. This means that each triangle has a pair of equal angles. By locating these angles in the drawing, it is possible to see that angle C comprises one angle equal to angle A and one angle equal to angle B. The sum of the three angles (A, B, and C) is 180 degrees, because they make up the large triangle ABC. Because angle C must be the same as angle A plus angle B, the measure of angle C must be exactly half of the 180 degrees, or 90 degrees. Mr. Eisner leads students through this proof step by step, asking students to respond to short-answer questions along the way.

Reviewing the Topic. It is now thirty-five minutes into the lesson, and Mr. Eisner hands out two pages summarizing the Law of Thales and its history. He selects students to read aloud small sections of the handout and asks if there are questions.

Assigning Homework. The lesson concludes with the assignment of homework. The problems require finding the measure of missing angles. Some involve the Law of Thales, some a review of previous work. Mr. Eisner asks if there are any questions about the problems, then says, "Okay. You can start with that until the bell." One minute later, forty-five minutes after the lesson began (about average for a German lesson), the bell rings.

A Japanese Lesson: Structured Problem Solving
From an American point of view, the Japanese lesson begins in a rather striking way. At the signal from the student monitor, all the students stand and bow, in unison, to the teacher. The teacher bows in return, and the lesson is officially under way.

Reviewing Yesterday's Lesson. After the customary exchange of bows, the students sit down and engage in a bit of joking with Mr. Yoshida, the teacher, about the video camera. Mr. Yoshida begins the lesson by reviewing the conclusion of the previous day's lesson. He notes that they had been working with "the relationship between parallel lines" and had ended by doing some problems. "Do you remember what they were?" he asks. There is no response, so he asks the students to get out the worksheet and look again at the first problem, which asked them to find the measure of the angle marked with an "x" in the drawing below. "We hurried through this problem," he says, "and were not able to summarize it well." Several solution methods had been presented, but briefly, and Mr. Yoshida asks the students to look again at the problem and finish it "with the method you think is easiest. . . . If you can give an explanation, that would be terrific."

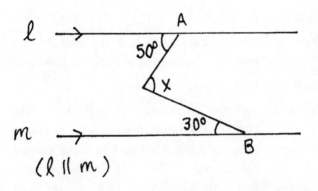

After two minutes, he asks the students to present what they have found. Three different methods are presented by students, all based on drawing an additional line segment. In some cases, a triangle is formed and students then use what they already know about measures of triangles to find the measure of angle x. After each presentation, Mr. Yoshida asks how many students used that procedure. He concludes this ten-minute segment by summarizing each of the three methods, pointing out the usefulness of drawing additional lines when finding the measures of some angles.

Presenting the Problem for the Day. The lesson continues with the problem for the day.

Mr. Yoshida:	Today, the problems cannot be solved without auxiliary lines. We want to do problems of this kind. The way the previous problem was made was to bend once between the parallel lines. Today, by changing this condition, I want you to make up your own problems. We won't change the parallel lines but how the angles look in the middle.
Mochida:	Outside?
Mr. Yoshida:	Oh, it's okay to go outside the lines. It is even okay to bend twice. I don't want you to bend ten times.
Students:	(Laughter)
Mr. Yoshida:	Twice or three times, that's the limit. After that, nobody will understand it. . . . Be creative. . . . One problem is okay, but if it's easy, do two problems. . . . Put in the angles by yourselves and write which angle is x. . . . It's pretty hard to put in the degrees. You can't just put in any degrees. . . . When you turn it in, you must be able to solve it. If people say they do not understand it, you must be able to explain it. Please think about it to the best of your abilities.

Working on the Problem Individually. As in the German lesson, the teacher presents a problem to the students that is mathematically challenging for eighth-graders. What is different is that Mr. Yoshida now asks the students to work out the solutions on their own rather than leading the class in developing the solution. Of course, students already have learned some methods that will help them get started.

For the next ten minutes, the students work individually on

constructing a problem for their peers to solve and on making sure they can solve it themselves. Mr. Yoshida circulates around the room, answering questions and giving hints. He appears increasingly concerned that students are not making more progress and finally says, "Well, it seems it was a little hard. I made a mistake. There are many of you that are in trouble. . . . Get in your groups, and from the problems you have made, pick a problem you and the others think is challenging, and group leaders please bring them up. Please check if the problem really can be solved and then bring it up."

Working on the Problem in Groups. As the students rearrange their desks, they move around the room and joke with one another about how hard the problems are that they have constructed. The noise gradually subsides, and after about two minutes, the leaders of the groups begin bringing up their problems for Mr. Yoshida to diagram on the chalkboard. After Mr. Yoshida records one problem for each of the six groups (see the diagrams below), he says, "These are the problems. We don't know whether we can solve them or not until we try. . . . It seems impossible to do all of them in this lesson, so we'll think about them a little next time, too. Please hurry and copy the six problems."

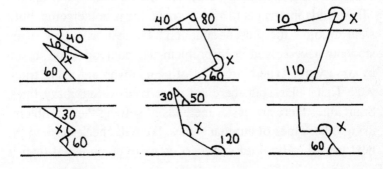

As students copy the problems, Mr. Yoshida walks around the room, observing students' work and commenting periodically about how difficult the students have made some of the problems. It soon becomes apparent that the students are trying to solve the problems as they copy them. Mr. Yoshida might have intended this, and he certainly does not discourage it. The students are still sitting in their groups; some are working together as a group, some are working in pairs, and some are working individually. After about ten minutes, Mr. Yoshida asks how many students have solved each of the problems. He then continues to circulate around the room, mostly observing as students continue to work.

Students have been working at their seats, either individually or in small groups, for about twenty minutes now, an unusually long segment of seatwork for a Japanese lesson, and they will continue in this way for another nine minutes. As the students continue to work, they occasionally raise their hands and ask Mr. Yoshida to look at what they have done. It is apparent that some students become excited at finding solutions to the problems that Mr. Yoshida identified as being especially difficult. Mr. Yoshida studies their solutions but refuses to comment on whether they are correct.

Summarizing the Main Point. The period is almost over, and Mr. Yoshida interrupts to say, "I know this is bothersome, but I want to know the present situation." He then asks how many students have solved each problem. He concludes the lesson by observing, "There are a lot of people who are using triangles. That's okay, but there are three types of auxiliary lines. Sometimes there are easier methods of solving these problems using other types of auxiliary lines. We will check these in the next period." His brief summary is more compressed than is typical for a Japanese lesson. The bell has already rung, forty-nine minutes after the lesson began (near average for a Japanese lesson), and the students now push their chairs back, stand, and bow.

A U.S. Lesson: Learning Terms and Practicing Procedures

Warming Up. The video begins with Mr. Jones, the teacher, conducting a "warm-up" activity. He points to the top left-hand drawing on the chalkboard (shown below).

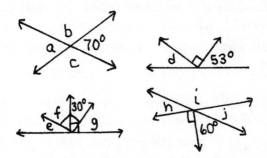

Mr. Jones:	What is the angle vertical to the seventy-degree angle? *(Pause)* John?
John:	I don't know.
Mr. Jones:	Don't get nervous *(apparently referring to the presence of the video camera).* When I intersect lines I get vertical angles. Right? Look at your definitions. I gave them to you. You can look them up. Here we have vertical angles and supplementary angles. Angle A is vertical to which angle?
Students:	Seventy (in chorus).
Mr. Jones:	Therefore angle A must be?

Students: Seventy degrees (in chorus).

Mr. Jones: Seventy degrees. Go from there. Now you have
               supplementary angles, don't you? What angle is
               supplementary to angle B?

Checking Homework. After five minutes of this quick-paced review, Mr. Jones asks the students to "get out the worksheet I gave earlier in the week and make sure we understand complementary, supplementary, and angle measurements." The class goes over the worksheet in a similar way: Mr. Jones asks students for answers and continues questioning them until they give the correct answer. The class checks thirty-six problems on the worksheet during six minutes of question-and-answer interaction.

Demonstrating Procedures. Reviewing previous work by checking homework is reminiscent of the German lesson. But the next activity is quite different from both the German and the Japanese lessons. Rather than presenting a topic or problem for the day, Mr. Jones distributes a worksheet that contains problems that, he notes, are "just like the warm-up." At the top of the worksheet is a sample problem with the solution and a suggested method shown. Mr. Jones takes a minute to go over this with the students and then asks if there are any questions. There are none, and the students begin working independently.

Practicing the Procedures. The worksheet contains forty problems, and the students spend the next eleven minutes working on them. The problems, like the homework and the warm-up, emphasize terms and procedures—in this case, finding the measures of complementary, supplementary, and vertical angles. Mr. Jones circulates around the room, answering questions and giving hints.

The lesson clearly has taken a different turn from those in Germany and Japan. The mathematics is quite simple compared with that found in the previous two lessons. But more than that, the teaching method is different. In the German lesson, the teacher led the students through the development of some advanced mathematical procedures. In the U.S. lesson, the development is limited to a quick demonstration. As in the Japanese lesson, students in the U.S. classroom spend the heart of the lesson working on assigned problems. But American students are asked to practice the demonstrated procedures on many simple problems rather than to develop procedures for solving a few challenging problems.

As Mr. Jones walks around the room, he begins receiving questions about problems 37 and 38. Apparently believing he should intervene when students are struggling or become confused, Mr. Jones goes to the chalkboard and works these two problems with the whole class. He begins with problem 38: "Write an equation that represents the sentence: The product of 12 and a number K is 192." Mr. Jones writes "12K" on the board and asks students what to write next. One student says "Equal sign," and Mr. Jones completes the equation: "12K = 192."

It might strike the reader as curious that this task has nothing to do with the day's lesson (calculating the measures of angles), but some American curriculum materials include review of earlier topics in later problem sets. In fact, it is not uncommon to find this kind of topic switch during U.S. lessons.

The discussion then turns to problem 37: "Angle QRS has the same measure as its supplement. Find m < QRS." Mr. Jones shows that the answer must be 90 degrees. Even these two problems, which were perceived to be the most difficult on the worksheet, are quite simple compared with those encountered by the German and Japanese students.

Demonstrating More Procedures. Mr. Jones gives the students two more minutes to finish the worksheet and then asks them to get out the worksheet they completed the previous Friday, after a quiz. One of the problems asked students to measure the interior angles of a hexagon (shown below) and compute the total. Mr. Jones asks if everyone got an answer close to 720 degrees. He then proceeds to the second part of the problem.

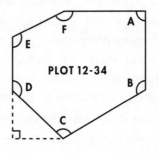

Mr. Jones:	If I took this angle (D) and moved it down here, and made it across this way *(see dotted lines in drawing),* moved D down here, should that change the sum, the total?
Jason:	No. *(Other students repeat this answer.)*
Mr. Jones:	It should not. Why? I still have how many angles?
Obed:	You still have six.

(It must be noted here that, based on what students have studied to this point, there is no way they can know the answer to

Mr. Jones's opening question, or that the number of angles is the crucial fact in finding the sum of the angle measures. But the nature and tone of teachers' questions often give away the answer, and a number of students apparently picked up on these cues and answered the questions appropriately.)

Mr. Jones:	I still have six angles. There is a formula, and we are going to go through this after spring break, but I will give you a hint right now. If I take the number of sides, and I subtract two, and I multiply that number times one hundred eighty degrees, that will tell me how many degrees these add up to. How many sides in this figure? *(Pause)*. Six. Right? Number of sides subtract two, gives me what?
Students:	Four.
Mr. Jones:	Four. What is four times one hundred eighty degrees?
Jacquille:	Seven hundred twenty.
Mr. Jones:	Should be seven hundred twenty, right? How many degrees should there be in a five-sided figure? *(Pause)*. Take the formula; the number of sides is five . . . subtract two, and multiply by one hundred eighty degrees.
Mike:	Five hundred ninety?
Mr. Jones:	Five hundred forty degrees. All five-sided figures contain five hundred forty degrees.

By giving the students this formula, Mr. Jones has just taken a problem that could have been challenging for the students (at a level similar to that in Germany and Japan) and changed it into a routine problem for which they must simply follow a rule. One of the features that make this lesson typical of teaching in the United States is just this: stating rules, rather than developing procedures, and thereby turning mathematics into a matter of following rules and practicing procedures.

Reviewing Procedures and Definitions. After using the formula to calculate the sum of the interior angles in a triangle, Mr. Jones makes several announcements about upcoming activities and future quizzes and tests. He then conducts a quick oral review with the class on the meaning of terms such as complementary, supplementary, obtuse angle, and acute angle. A few minutes remain, and Mr. Jones tells the students to use the time "to finish up any of this, and ask me questions." The lesson ends with a bell, forty-eight minutes after it began (about average for the United States).

Variations on a Theme

After watching these lessons, and many others like them, we developed the images of teaching, complete with mottoes, that we sketched at the beginning of this chapter. But we noted then that these images are, in many ways, too simplistic. Why? Because there is a range of lessons in each country. Many lessons look much like the ones we have described, and it is from these that the simple images were formed. But some lessons look quite different. We can form richer images of teaching by seeing the full spectrum of lessons.

German Variations: More Practice and More Student Participation

The spectrum of lessons in Germany moves out from the center in two different directions. Some lessons focus more on practicing skills already learned than does the lesson taught by Mr. Eisner; other lessons include more student exploration of concepts and procedures.

Practicing skills is illustrated by a lesson on solving linear equations. The lesson begins with the teacher reporting that the students' performance on a recent test was not very good and suggesting that more practice is needed. The teacher asks two students to come to the chalkboard, and he dictates a problem for each of them. The first problem is $(2x - 3)/3 - (3x + 4)/4 = -9/20 - (4x - 3)/5$. The rest of the students are expected to watch and correct errors as the two students work through the problems at the chalkboard. The teacher carefully monitors the step-by-step procedures of both students, often asking questions and correcting errors. After the two students finish, the teacher asks if there are questions and calls two more students to the front, dictating two new problems. The entire lesson proceeds in the same way. Some aspects of the lesson are quite typical: students working on complex procedures at the chalkboard with the teacher monitoring progress; and the teacher orchestrating a whole-class question-and-answer discussion of the solutions. But the emphasis on skills already learned, without the development of a new concept, is different from most lessons.

The second kind of variation—more student participation in developing the mathematics—is illustrated by the following lesson. The teacher begins by reviewing the main point from the previous lesson: special polygons, like squares and equilateral triangles, are defined by special relationships and special properties of their sides, angles, and so on. The teacher then distributes cardboard models of a variety of special polygons and asks the students to find all of the special properties they can—sizes and relationships of sides and angles, and axes of symmetry. Students work together in small groups, and after about fifteen minutes group representatives come to the front, one at a time, and fill in the cells of a large chart, answering "yes" or "no" to statements such as "sides are equal," "angles are equal," and "diagonals are axes of symmetry" with respect to their polygon. One polygon, the kite, creates considerable disagreement among the students. The teacher demonstrates again how to check special properties and asks everyone to reexamine the kite.

As we put together the typical features with the variations, our image of German mathematics teaching as "developing advanced procedures" still seems appropriate. In Mr. Eisner's lesson, the procedures were methods for proving the Law of Thales, a powerful and rich theorem in geometry. The two variations can be interpreted as complements to the theme. In one case, the emphasis shifts from the initial development of procedures to proficiency of execution. In the second case, the teacher allows the students to participate more directly in the development of the procedures, at least for a short time. But the teacher is still in control, carefully constraining the task to ensure certain outcomes. Both kinds of variation support the image of the knowledgeable teacher leading students through the development of advanced mathematical procedures.

Japanese Variations: Teacher Telling and Students Memorizing

At first glance, the variations we find in Japanese lessons appear to conflict sharply with the lesson presented by Mr.

Yoshida. It is not even clear that the typical lessons and the variations fit along the same spectrum. We see teachers lecturing about a topic or telling students how to solve a problem or asking students to memorize properties or facts through repeated recitation. It is especially interesting that when these activities occur, they often are put together, in the same lesson, with students' solving problems and sharing solution methods. From an American point of view, this looks rather odd.

In one lesson, the teacher begins by identifying the new topic that will continue for several weeks—the analysis of polygons. For the next thirty-five minutes, he lectures. He talks about historical discoveries, about the prevalence of these figures in the real world, and about the fact that this topic is more closely related to the previous one—linear functions—than students might think, because both search for relationships. He concludes by posting the goal for mathematics: "To learn to think logically while searching for new properties and relationships." He asks students to repeat this goal several times and memorize it. The teacher then says that the first task will be to study relationships among angles, and he draws a large X on the board. He asks students to draw a similar X on their papers and to use a protractor to investigate the relationships among the angles. "Write down things you notice," he says. After five minutes the students share what they've found, including that the angles opposite each other are equal. The teacher wonders aloud whether this would always be true. Could it be proved? He then, with large hints, helps students discover a proof.

In another lesson, the teacher begins by reviewing three properties of parallelograms that they have developed thus far, such as "opposite sides are of equal length." He posts the three statements, and the students spend fifteen minutes reciting them. The class recites them together, then a student stands and recites them alone, then they spend one minute reciting them quietly to themselves, and then they repeat the process. The teacher concludes this activity by saying that students need to remember the properties because they will need them. He then presents the picture shown below and says, "If ABCD is a parallelogram and BE equals DF, prove that AE equals CF." The proof, not surprisingly, uses the properties just recited, and the students are asked to develop and share several different proofs.

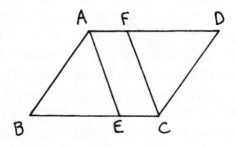

At first glance, these two lessons look quite different from the one taught by Mr. Yoshida. But after viewing them several times, we can see how they complement the image of "structured problem solving." When students are asked to solve challenging problems, teachers often build scaffolds to help them. The scaffolds come in many forms. Sometimes they are the outcomes of previous lessons, reviewed by the teacher (as in Mr. Yoshida's lesson). Sometimes they are in the form of information provided through lectures, and sometimes in the form of mental tools provided through memorization. What is constant is that challenging problems are selected and scaffolds are provided so that students can, at the least, begin developing methods for solution.

Not every lesson, however, fits neatly along this spectrum. In one lesson, the teacher says that today they will be talking about the solutions and graphs for simultaneous linear equations. She then leads the students through a twenty-five-minute review of graphing linear equations, showing them how they can translate any form to $y = mx + b$ and can then graph the equation easily. She then shows that when two equations are graphed on the same axes, they often intersect in one point, and this point is special—it has coordinates that satisfy both equations. Throughout the entire discussion, she asks students short-answer questions and accepts their responses, but she essentially tells the students what they need to know and how to solve the problems.

This lesson shows that "structured problem solving" does not capture the full range of Japanese instruction. Indeed, it seems that the teaching method in this lesson is more like the methods typically used in Germany than the methods typically used in Japan. If nothing else, the lesson reminds us that not all teachers within the same country use the same methods.

U.S. Variations: More Review and More Student Participation

As in Germany, the spectrum of lessons in the United States moves out from the most common in two different directions: even more review than in Mr. Jones's lesson on one side, and more student participation on the other.

In one lesson, the teacher announces that students will have time to review for the upcoming chapter test. Apparently referring to the suggestions in the teacher's manual, the teacher says, "What they said is that I shouldn't review with you; you should do it in your groups." The students begin reviewing. Although their desks are placed together in groups of four, most students work through the textbook review page on their own, raising their hands when they have questions. The teacher circulates around the room for the full period, answering questions and briefly tutoring individual students who need help.

Another lesson, although also review, contrasts sharply in teaching method. The teacher hands back the previous day's quiz as each student enters the room. The teacher asks the students to get into their groups and compare responses, check mistakes they made, and decide to present one problem to the class that was hard for them. During most of the lesson, group representatives, in turn, present their selections on the chalkboard and lead a class discussion about methods of solution. One problem is to solve the following systems of equations: $y = 2x - 9$; $x + 2y = 2$. Another problem is to factor $8x^2 + 8$. Apparently, the teacher intends for students to present and discuss their methods, but she often jumps in to correct or explain or cut off discussion in order to move to the next problem. At the end of the lesson, the teacher reviews the slope-intercept form for linear equations and how it can be used to construct graphs, and then assigns twenty-five problems from the textbook for homework.

Both kinds of variations, in different ways, are consistent with our simplified U.S. image of "learning terms and practicing procedures." The first kind of variation—additional review—simply reinforces the theme. The second kind of variation expands the image. Although the goal of the second lesson is similar to the goal of the others—learn terms and practice procedures—the classroom activities in which the students are engaged look quite different. Working with other students to analyze problems, presenting problems to the class, describing one's own method for solving them, and asking questions of peers—all these give students a more active role than they had in either the review lesson or Mr. Jones's classroom.

Lessons in which students participate in this way might show the effects of the current reform efforts. There are, however, very few of these lessons, and when they do occur, the variations from the theme appear in the *form* of activities, not the substance. Students are seen working in small groups or engaging in a discussion about solution methods, but the mathematics is simple compared with that encountered by their German and Japanese peers, and the work and discussion are mostly about memorizing definitions for terms and following rules and procedures.

Can We Trust the Images?

Portraits of individual lessons are useful when they create images of teaching that represent the way teaching actually looks. But they can be dangerous if they misrepresent the situation. It is wise to be skeptical when deciding whether the description of a few lessons creates a fair image of teaching in each country. This is especially true when dealing with activities as complex as classroom teaching.

Of course, we presented these typical lessons because we believe that they *are* useful. They capture quite well the images of teaching that we formed while watching the tapes and discussing them with our colleagues, and we believe they are a fair representation of teaching in each country. But as we stated at the end of Chapter 2, both impressionistic reports and coded data are necessary for learning about teaching. By examining the coded data from the lessons, readers can check the claims we made about what is typical in each country. The coded data also help to refine these images of teaching. In the next chapter, we present this information and then come to some fundamental conclusions about the nature of teaching, regardless of what it looks like or where you find it.

CHAPTER 4

Refining the Images

O NE OF THE ADVANTAGES of comparing activities across
cultures is that we can see things we might never
have noticed had we looked only within our own culture. This was illustrated one day early in the study, as we sat
with our colleagues watching a U.S. lesson. The teacher in the
video was standing at the chalkboard, in the midst of demonstrating a procedure, when a voice came over the public
address system: "May I have your attention, please. All students riding in bus thirty-one, you will meet your bus in the
rear of the school today, not in the front of the school. Teachers please take note of this and remind your students."

A Japanese member of our team reached over and pushed
STOP on the VCR. "What was that?" he asked. "Oh, nothing,"
we replied as we pushed the PLAY button. "Wait," protested our
Japanese colleague. "What do you mean, nothing?" As we
patiently tried to explain that it was just a P.A. announcement,
he became more and more incredulous. Were we implying that
it was normal to interrupt a lesson? How could that ever happen? Such interruptions would never happen in Japan, he said,
because they would ruin the flow of the lesson. As he went on,

we began to wonder whether this interruption was more significant than we had thought.

But wait. Before we rush to interpret these interruptions, how sure are we that the countries really differ significantly on this score? The brief interaction with our Japanese colleague demonstrates the way images like those developed in the previous chapter can begin to form. But it also shows how easy it would be to build images that turn out to be invalid. How often are U.S. lessons really interrupted, and how infrequent are such interruptions in Japan? Fortunately, we do not have to rely on images alone to guide our understanding of how classrooms look in different cultures.

In this chapter we look across all the lessons and ask whether these images hold up for the full sample. How often do teachers just state concepts or procedures rather than develop them? In what percentage of lessons do students just practice procedures versus doing creative mathematical work? How different is the mathematical content presented by teachers in the three countries? By using the coded data we can answer questions like these and refine our images of teaching in each country.

Mathematics in the Classroom

One of the most striking impressions when watching the videotapes is that students in the United States encounter a different kind of mathematics from that encountered by their peers in Germany and Japan. The content appears to be less advanced and is presented in a more piecemeal and prescriptive way. We wanted to test these impressions, because the level and nature of the content to which students are exposed set boundaries on students' learning opportunities. If the content is rich and challenging, it is more likely that students have the opportunity to learn more mathematics and to learn it more deeply. If the content is fragmented and ordinary, students have less chance of learning important mathematics. In this section, we look at three indicators of content: its level of difficulty, how extensively it is developed, and how coherently it is presented.

Level of Content

It is very difficult to say how advanced or difficult particular mathematics content is from the students' point of view, because that depends on how well students have been prepared to deal with the topic, how it is presented, what is expected of them, and so on. But we can tell how advanced a topic is, on the international yardstick, by finding where it is placed in mathematics curricula around the world. As part of the Third International Mathematics and Science Study (TIMSS), William Schmidt and his colleagues at Michigan State University conducted an analysis of the grade level at which the majority of the forty-one TIMSS countries gave the most concentrated attention to each mathematical topic.[1]

The topics treated in the eighth-grade videotaped lessons were matched against this scale. The United States lagged significantly behind Germany and Japan.[2] By international standards, the mathematical content of the U.S. lessons was, on average, at a mid-seventh-grade level, whereas German and Japanese lessons were at the high eighth- and beginning ninth-grade levels, respectively. This means that most eighth-graders in the United States study topics that students in many other countries encounter a year earlier.

Despite the obvious importance of this finding, it cannot by itself explain the relatively poor achievement of American students. German eighth-graders were more than one year ahead of U.S. students in the level of content they were studying, yet their performance on the achievement test was not significantly higher than that of the American eighth-graders.[3] Challenging content alone does not lead to high achievement. The same content can be taught deeply or superficially. Students learning to solve algebraic equations might be asked to grapple with such deep mathematical concepts as variables, functions, and equivalence. On the other hand, they might simply be taught to mechanically follow the steps for solving equations. Students' learning of algebra will differ depending on how the content is taught.

Nature of Content

One of the reasons we dubbed American teaching "learning terms and practicing procedures" is that lessons in the United States seemed to place greater emphasis on definitions of terms and less emphasis on underlying rationale. When we counted the number of definitions presented in all lessons, we found that there were about twice as many in the United States as in Germany or Japan.

Of course, there is nothing wrong with presenting definitions in mathematics; in fact, definitions are necessary. Knowing what the terms mean is crucial for communicating about mathematics. What matters most, however, is what one does with definitions. If students simply learn definitions to increase their mathematical vocabulary, they are just scratching the mathematical surface. If students use definitions to explore the deeper properties and relationships in mathematics, then they really are doing mathematics.

Students in Mr. Jones's class, the lesson we portrayed as typical of the United States, were learning definitions of terms such as "supplementary angles" and "complementary angles" (two angles are supplementary if they form a straight line; that is, if their measures add up to 180 degrees). Problems in Mr. Jones's lesson involved finding, for example, the supplement of a 70-degree angle. Definitions were the beginning and the end of the mathematics. In contrast, the problem in one of the Japanese lessons asked students to look for relationships among the angles formed when drawing an X. By *using* the definition of supplementary angles, a proof was developed to show that vertical angles are always equal. This treatment of mathematics goes much beyond learning a definition.

One way to tell how deeply the mathematics is being developed is to look at the kind of reasoning that was required. In Mr. Eisner's lesson, the task required deductive reasoning, a hallmark of mathematical thinking. One begins with a statement that is accepted as true and builds a logical chain of observations to reach a conclusion that is, necessarily, true. In mathematics, deductive reasoning is often found in proofs. As it turns out, there were *no* mathematical proofs in U.S. lessons. In contrast, there were proofs in 53 percent of Japanese lessons and 10 percent of German lessons. Whatever students in the United States were doing with the definitions, they clearly were not using them to develop proofs of mathematical relationships.

Content Elaboration

Most mathematics lessons include the presentation of concepts, either by the teacher or by the students. We used the label "concepts" broadly to apply to all instances in which information was presented by explaining an idea, by demonstrating an idea with an example, or simply by stating the information. We were interested in whether concepts were just stated or whether they were developed. As was described in Chapter 3, Mr. Jones *stated* the formula for the sum of the angles in a polygon, and Mr. Eisner *developed* the Law of Thales. How common is this difference among countries?

To answer this question, we first divided the lessons into topic segments. Topics were defined by the TIMSS curriculum analysis referred to earlier: items such as linear measurement, ratio and proportion, division of decimals, and so on. Then we analyzed whether the concepts within each topic were developed or just stated. We defined "developed" quite generously to include cases in which the concept was explained or illustrated, even with a few sentences or a brief example. We found that one-fifth of the topics in U.S. lessons contained developed concepts, while four-fifths contained only stated concepts. As is shown in Figure 4.1, this distribution was nearly reversed in Germany and Japan. These data add more weight to the impression that students in Germany and Japan have richer opportunities to learn the meanings behind the formulas and procedures they are acquiring.

Content Coherence

One observation we made in Chapter 3, almost as an aside, was that the mathematics seemed to be more fragmented in the U.S. lesson, as evidenced by a curious shift of topics. Students in Mr. Jones's class spent most of their time considering the measures of angles, but one problem asked them to "Write an equation that represents the sentence: The product of 12 and a number K is 192." The problem had nothing to do with the main lesson topic. Was this an aberration? Does it matter?

By itself, the event is not very significant. But it raises the question of lesson coherence—the connectedness or relatedness of the mathematics across the lesson. And coherence *is*

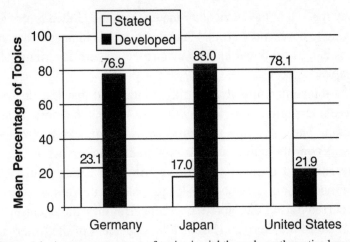

Figure 4.1. Average percentage of topics in eighth-grade mathematics lessons that contained concepts that were DEVELOPED or STATED.
Source: U.S. Department of Education, National Center for Education Statistics, Third International Mathematics and Science Study, Videotape Classroom Study, 1994–95.

significant. Imagine the lesson as a story. Well-formed stories consist of a sequence of events that fit together to reach the final conclusion. Ill-formed stories are scattered sets of events that don't seem to connect. As readers know, well-formed stories are easier to comprehend than ill-formed stories. And well-formed stories are like coherent lessons. They offer the students greater opportunities to make sense of what is going on.[4]

Threats to Coherence. One way to measure coherence is to look for threats to coherence, features of lessons that make it difficult to design and sustain a smoothly developing story. Threats include things like switching topics frequently, or as we noted at the beginning of this chapter, being interrupted by outside intrusions. We found that U.S. lessons contained significantly more topics than did Japanese lessons, and significantly more switches from topic to topic than both German and Japanese lessons. This may mean that the curriculum materials in the United States are trying to cover more ground than the materials in the other countries but, as we found in the previous section, are covering it less deeply.[5]

As for interruptions, we did, in fact, find that U.S. lessons were interrupted more frequently than lessons in Germany and Japan. The interruptions came from things like announcements over the public address system and visitors who entered the room to request something, like the lunch count. As claimed by our Japanese colleague, such interruptions never occurred during the Japanese lessons. But they did occur in 13 percent of the German lessons and 31 percent of the American lessons.

Making Connections. Threats to coherence tell only part of the story. Coherence is achieved through weaving together ideas and activities. One way to help students notice how ideas are related is to explicitly point out the connections among them. For example, several minutes into a German lesson, the teacher said, "Next is a step you really need to pay close attention to because we're dealing here with different numbers from those we dealt with yesterday." The teacher went on to elaborate the differences and at the same time point out connections between the previous day's work and the current day's activities. Connections can also be made between ideas within lessons. Halfway through a U.S. lesson on solving sets of linear equations, the teacher asked the students to consider an alternative procedure and related it to a point made early in the lesson: "What might have been the other choice? What would have been the logical choice that just had the two terms? This is what Hugh was talking about at the beginning, where you have just a square term and a constant."

We found that although the majority of teachers in all countries made explicit links from one lesson to another, only the Japanese teachers routinely linked together the parts of a lesson. In fact, 96 percent of Japanese lessons contained explicit statements by the teacher connecting one part of the lesson with another, whereas only 40 percent of German and U.S. lessons contained such statements.

Other judgments about coherence, such as the flow of mathematical connections, are quite subtle and require a good deal of mathematical sophistication. So we asked a group of four university mathematics teachers (we'll call them the Math Group) to analyze the lessons.[6] We asked them to devise a means of systematically describing the mathematical content of each lesson along dimensions that they thought were relevant for student learning. What they found is both interesting and important.

The Math Group worked from written descriptions of the lessons that contained information on how the lesson was organized, what activities were used, what tasks were presented, the solution strategies that were presented by the teacher and the students, and so on. One advantage of using these written charts rather than the videotapes was that country-specific references, such as coin systems or students' names, could be disguised so that the Math Group did not know which lesson was from which country. To reduce the immensity of their task, we gave them a subset of lessons to analyze: fifteen geometry and fifteen algebra lessons, randomly chosen from each country, for a total of ninety lessons.

As they studied the charts, the Math Group began mapping out the mathematical ideas in different parts of each lesson and how they were related. For example, in Mr. Yoshida's lesson (Chapter 3), students first reviewed finding the measures of angles by drawing auxiliary lines. Then they were asked to construct their own problems that could be solved using auxiliary lines. This segment was related to the previous one in a number of ways: (1) it was *similar* to the first segment with respect to the basic mathematical ideas; (2) it was *dependent* on the first segment procedurally—students could apply the methods they used in the first segment to begin creating and solving their problems; and (3) it *extended* the first segment procedurally and conceptually by increasing the complexity of the problems.

In Mr. Jones's lesson, students first reviewed complementary, supplementary, and vertical angles. Then they spent most of the lesson solving problems that were similar. "Just like the warm-up," said Mr. Jones. "All . . . are done the same way." Although most segments of the lesson were related, because the problems were similar, in terms of content there were fewer mathematical relationships from one segment to the next. For example, there was no increase in mathematical complexity from the beginning of the lesson to the end.

The Math Group captured these kinds of differences by mapping out all of the mathematical relationships between segments of lessons. They reported their results in two ways. First, they counted the number of lessons in which all segments were connected through at least one appropriate mathematical relationship. Using our story analogy, these were lessons that told a single story. Of the thirty lessons analyzed from each country, 45 percent of the U.S. lessons, 76 percent of the German lessons, and 92 percent of the Japanese lessons fit this criterion.

Then the Math Group calculated a summary score for each lesson to indicate the degree to which the parts of the lesson were interrelated. By this measure, German lessons scored four times as high as U.S. lessons. Japanese lessons scored six times as high as U.S. lessons.

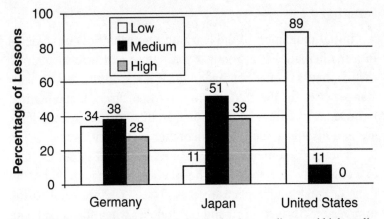

Figure 4.2. Percentage of lessons rated as having low, medium, and high quality of mathematical content.
Source: U.S. Department of Education, National Center for Education Statistics, Third International Mathematics and Science Study, Videotape Classroom Study, 1994–95.

Overall Quality of Content. The Math Group conducted one final analysis. They assessed the overall quality of the mathematics in each lesson with regard to its potential for helping students understand important mathematics. This subjective judgment was, of course, related to coherence, but it also took into account the two aspects of mathematics we considered earlier—the level of challenge and how the content was developed. The Math Group sorted the lessons into three quality categories: low, medium, and high. Remember, they did not know which lessons came from which countries. The results are shown in Figure 4.2. In the judgment of these experienced mathematicians and mathematics teachers, American students were at a clear disadvantage in their opportunities to learn, at least as indicated by the mathematics content of their lessons.

Summary

An initial indication of the learning opportunities for students in a mathematics classroom is the nature and level of mathematics that is on the playing field. What is in the lesson, substance-wise, for the students to use to construct mathematical knowledge? We have learned that, in this regard, U.S. students are at a disadvantage. They encounter mathematics that is at a lower level, is somewhat more superficial, and is not as fully or coherently developed as the mathematics encountered by their German and Japanese peers. These findings add to the impressions formed in Chapter 3. Indeed, when the coded data are examined, differences in the content of the lessons appear to be even larger than when individual lessons are compared. U.S. students encounter less-challenging mathematics, and because it is presented in a less-coherent way, they must work harder to make sense of it than their peers in Germany and Japan. Still, this is not the whole story.

Engaging Students in Mathematics

Differences among the lessons of Messrs. Eisner, Yoshida, and Jones seemed to lie in more than just the content. The way in which students were asked to engage in mathematics seemed to be different. In the German and U.S. lessons, students participated mostly by giving brief responses to the teacher's specific questions. Although the level of mathematics was higher in Germany, in both countries the teacher did most of the mathematical work. In Japan, the reverse seemed to be true. The typical Japanese lesson invited students to do more of the mathematical work. How prevalent are these characteristics of lessons in each country?

Lesson Organization

The way a lesson is organized provides a shell, or context, within which the teacher engages students in learning the subject. All the teachers tended to divide their lessons into periods of classwork and seatwork. Classwork is when the teacher is working with all the students and, usually, orchestrating the discussion. Activities include learning a new concept, reviewing a previously learned concept or procedure, solving a problem together, or sharing solution methods for problems that have been solved. Seatwork is the time when students work individually or in small groups on assigned tasks. Talk is mostly private—teacher-student or student-student.

Teachers in all three countries spent more time in classwork than in seatwork. In Japan and the United States 60 percent of the time was spent in classwork; in Germany, it was 70 percent. Although the overall percentage of time spent in classwork was similar, shifts within the lesson from classwork to seatwork and vice versa were considerably more frequent in Japan than in the other two countries. As a consequence, the duration of segments defined by classroom organization tended to be shorter in Japan than in the other countries.

The full meaning of lesson organization becomes clear when we examine what happens during classwork and seatwork. Who does the work, and what kind of work is being done?

Who Does the Work?

Many educators agree that learning opportunities are enhanced when students do most of the mathematics work during the lesson.[7] But just looking at whether things are being done during classwork or seatwork does not tell us enough. The teacher often is doing the work during classwork but might orchestrate the discussion so that students are required to do more of the work; students often are doing the work during seatwork but might be assigned tasks for which the teacher already has done the mental work. To measure more accurately who is doing the mathematical work, the Math Group looked at who controlled the solution method to a problem, the teacher or the students.

For example, Mr. Jones showed students the formula for finding the sum of the interior angles of a polygon: sum = $180°$ x (number of sides − 2). He then asked students to calculate the sums of various polygons. Students were to execute the formula; Mr. Jones controlled the method. The same problem could have been presented in a much different way. The teacher might have asked students to measure the sums of interior angles of various polygons using a protractor, and then try to find some patterns that would help them compute the sums more quickly. Students could have been given responsibility to work out various solution methods—including, perhaps, a general formula. Then students would have controlled the solution method.

The Math Group found that the tasks were predominantly student-controlled in 9 percent of the American lessons, 19 percent of the German lessons, and 40 percent of the Japanese lessons. Our impression is confirmed—students in the Japanese lessons did more of the mathematical work than students in the other countries.

What Kind of Work Is Expected?

One way to measure the kind of work students do is to apply the idea of student-controlled tasks and to look at whether students are asked to develop multiple solution methods for problems. Mathematical problems can have one right answer, but usually

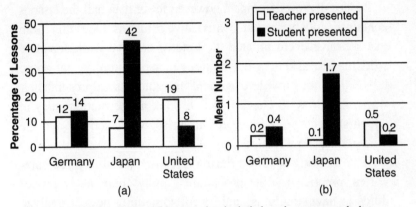

Figure 4.3. (a) Percentage of lessons that included student-presented alternative solution methods; (b) average number of student-presented alternative solution methods presented per lesson.
Source: U.S. Department of Education, National Center for Education Statistics, Third International Mathematics and Science Study, Videotape Classroom Study, 1994–95.

there are many ways to find the answer. For example, the problem in Mr. Jones's lesson—finding the sum of the measures of the interior angles of a polygon—can be solved by (1) measuring the angles of the particular polygon with a protractor and adding them up, or (2) measuring the angles of several polygons, looking for patterns, and predicting the answer, or (3) using the results of (2) to invent a formula. The fact that there are usually many ways to find an answer is important because it is generally agreed that richer, more conceptual learning opportunities are available if students are encouraged to examine the relative advantages of different methods,[8] and this is a place where students can participate in *doing* mathematics.

As was hinted at by the lessons described in Chapter 3, Japanese lessons included significantly more student-presented alternative solution methods than did German or American lessons (see Figure 4.3).

Notice that even in Japan, however, fewer than half the lessons contained student-presented alternative solutions. Does this mean that we have overestimated the kind of creative work Japanese students are asked to do, or does it mean simply that some lessons do not provide class time for students to present their work? One way to check this is to look at the mathematics in which students were engaged during seatwork activity and the kind of thinking it required.

The thinking required during seatwork fell into three categories: practice routine procedures, apply concepts or procedures in new situations, and invent something new or analyze situations in new ways. The first category is well known and was prevalent in Mr. Jones's class. He demonstrated, for example, how to identify and calculate supplementary angles and then assigned a number of practice exercises. The second category consists of situations in which students are encouraged to use a particular idea to solve a problem but it is not immediately obvious how this might be done. The third category contains tasks in which students must invent something or in which they were asked to think about and analyze a mathematical situation in a new way. In Mr. Yoshida's class, students were asked to invent new problems that could be solved using what they knew about angle measures.

As is shown in Figure 4.4, Japanese students spent about equal amounts of time practicing routine procedures and inventing something new, whereas German and American students spent almost all their time practicing routine procedures.

Summary

We have learned that students in Germany and the United States learn mathematics by following the teacher's lead. In Germany, this often takes the form of responding to specific

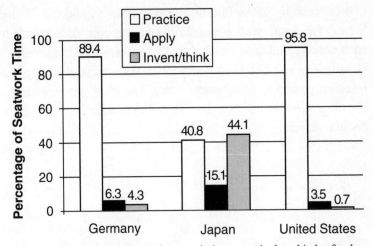

Figure 4.4. Average percentage of seatwork time spent in three kinds of tasks. *Source:* U.S. Department of Education, National Center for Education Statistics, Third International Mathematics and Science Study, Videotape Classroom Study, 1994–95.

questions from the teacher as the whole class develops a mathematical procedure. In the United States, this often takes the form of following the teacher's directions by practicing a procedure during seatwork.

Although Mr. Yoshida's lesson might make it tempting to say that the reverse is true in Japan, the data do not support this. A more accurate picture is that, on average, there is a balance in Japan. The mathematical work is shared by the teacher and the students. Students sometimes, but not always, do creative mathematical work by inventing new methods and presenting them to the class. At other times, teachers control the mathematics—lecturing, demonstrating, asking students to memorize, and so on.

Using the tools of both subjective impression and objective codes, we have now built a picture of what eighth-grade mathematics teaching looks like in Germany, Japan, and the United States. We began with some simple impressions of teaching in each country and then checked these impressions against national samples. We zeroed in on specific features of teaching—in research parlance, "indicators"—that might influence students' learning. Now let us examine what these indicators can tell us about teaching.

CHAPTER 5

Teaching Is a System

A LTHOUGH VIDEOTAPES are a rich source of information, they provide only glimpses of the full activity of teaching. We have found images of teaching in each country, and we have constructed indicators that measure the features of classroom lessons in each country. These images and indicators provide only partial views of teaching, however. It is as if we are seeing the peaks of mountain ranges poking above the surface of the water. The videotapes provide views of these mountaintop islands, but still hidden, underneath the surface, are the mountain ranges.

We discovered that mountain ranges lay beneath the surface as we asked ourselves why the indicators revealed certain differences among the countries. Consider the following simple indicator. Many mathematics teachers in the United States use an overhead projector, whereas almost all teachers in Japan prefer the chalkboard.[1] Some would say this is a trivial difference and not worth worrying about. But when we look more closely at this superficial difference we see that it points to a deeper, more significant difference in the way teaching is conducted.

When we look again at teachers using overhead projectors

and chalkboards, we begin to see that teachers in the two countries do not just use different visual devices, they use them in different ways. Most teachers in the United States use visual devices to focus students' attention. They use both overhead projectors and chalkboards to display information in written or graphic form while they are describing it orally. As they finish each part of their oral presentation, they often erase that part of the written material and move to the next item. Whether they use overhead projectors or chalkboards, they use these visual aids to keep students' attention directed toward the information of the moment. This observation is not a new revelation. Many preservice teacher-training programs offer advice on using overhead projectors in just this way. Readers who have participated in such teacher training might remember being told to cover up all the items on the transparency except the one being presented, then to move the cover down to the next item, and so on. When finished presenting the last item, the teacher is told to turn off the projector so as to reclaim students' attention.

Japanese teachers use visual aids for a very different purpose: to provide a record of the problems and solution methods and principles that are discussed during the lesson. The first item of information in the lesson is placed at the far left of the chalkboard; the next item, whether presented by a student or the teacher, is written next to it; and so on. The record builds, left to right, as the lesson proceeds. Many Japanese teachers finish the lesson with a full chalkboard, showing a complete record of the lesson.

The fact that U.S. teachers frequently use overhead projectors and Japanese teachers use only chalkboards indicates much more than a whimsical preference in visual aids. Given how these aids are employed in each culture, we can now see that Japanese teachers would *not* use overhead projectors, whereas U.S. teachers would use either one but probably would find overhead projectors more effective. Visual aids function very differently in these two different systems of teaching.

And here is the significant truth about teaching that this simple-seeming indicator reveals: teaching is a *system*. It is not a loose mixture of individual features thrown together by the teacher. It works more like a machine, with the parts operating together and reinforcing one another, driving the vehicle forward. In the U.S. machine, or system, there is a slot for a visual aid that helps focus students' attention. The overhead projector serves this purpose as well as, or better than, the chalkboard, so it is easy to see why many teachers have shifted to the overhead. In the Japanese system, there is no such slot. Instead, there is a slot for presenting a cumulative record of the day's lesson. The overhead projector does not function in this way, so Japanese teachers do not use it; they continue to use the chalkboard.[2]

If teaching is a system, then each feature, by itself, doesn't say much about the kind of teaching that is going on. What is important is how the features fit together to form a whole. How does one feature connect with the next one? How does an activity near the end of the lesson link back with one at the beginning? This is a very different way to think about teaching. It means that individual features make sense only in terms of how they relate with others that surround them. It means that most individual features, by themselves, are not good or bad. Their value depends on how they connect with others and fit into the lesson.

One lesson we described briefly in Chapter 3 began with pure memorization. The teacher asked students to recite three properties they had learned already about parallelograms, such as "opposite sides are parallel and of equal length." Individual students stood and recited them and were corrected by the teacher. The class recited them together. Students rehearsed them silently and then again recited them aloud. This continued for fifteen minutes. We wondered why the teacher was drilling the students so intensely. Some might see this as poor teaching—or at least as unnecessary.

Then the teacher told the students that they would be working on a problem for which they might find the properties useful. He presented a theorem about parallelograms and asked the students to prove it. As it turned out, the three properties they just had memorized were the key pieces they needed in order to work out a proof. Most students were reasonably successful. Now the memorization feature of the lesson took on new meaning for us. It fit well with the surrounding features and with the goal of the lesson.

Patterns of Teaching in Three Countries

Returning to our metaphor, we now became interested in discovering the nature of the mountain ranges that lay beneath the surface. How could we describe the systems of teaching in each country? We stepped back and watched the tapes again, looking for how the different pieces of the lesson fit together. The fact that we were watching lessons from different countries was invaluable.

Our perceptions of classroom lessons changed, depending on the context in which we viewed them. When we watched only U.S. lessons, we tended to notice the differences among them. Some teachers demonstrated a procedure by working through several examples in a lecture form, others by asking students to fill in steps, and still others by passing out reference sheets and talking through the worked examples with the students. Some teachers presented rather long demonstrations and then gave students the rest of the time to work on the assignment, whereas others gave a brief demonstration, asked students to work on a few similar problems, checked their progress, gave another demonstration, assigned a few more problems, and so on. Some teachers asked students to work on the assigned problems in small groups; others asked students to work individually. Differences in how the demonstration was handled and how teachers structured seatwork were aspects of the lessons that stood out.

When we watched a lesson from another country, we suddenly saw something different. Now we were struck by the similarity among the U.S. lessons and by how different they were from the other country's lesson. When we watched a Japanese lesson, for example, we noticed that the teacher presents a problem to the students without first demonstrating how to solve the problem. We realized that U.S. teachers almost never do this, and now we saw that a feature we hardly noticed before is perhaps one of the most important features of U.S. lessons—that the teacher almost always demonstrates a procedure for solving problems before assigning them to students. This is the value of cross-cultural comparisons. They allow us to detect the underlying commonalities that define particular systems of teaching, commonalities that otherwise hide in the background.

Through this process, we began to see something that surprised us: The systems of teaching within each country look similar from lesson to lesson. At least, there are certain recurring features that typify many of the lessons within a country and distinguish the lessons among countries. These recurring features, or *patterns,* define different parts of a lesson and the way the parts are sequenced. They serve as a kind of shorthand for the common teaching approach in each country and, metaphorically, begin to describe the nature of the mountain ranges underneath the visible islands.

The German Pattern

German lessons usually unfold through a sequence of four activities.

- *Reviewing previous material.* This can take several forms, including reviewing homework or reminding students what they have accomplished up to this point.
- *Presenting the topic and the problems for the day.* In Mr. Eisner's lesson, the topic was the measure of angles, and the problem was to prove that all angles inscribed in a semicircle measured 90 degrees.
- *Developing the procedures to solve the problem.* Mr. Eisner directed the development (in this case, of a proof) from the chalkboard. In some lessons, students are asked to work at the chalkboard, taking suggestions from other students and the teacher. When students work at the chalkboard, the teacher retains control of the development, even when positioned at the back of the room.
- *Practicing.* Usually, this is handled through the assignment of seatwork, which can become homework if not finished. The problems often are similar to those that have been worked during the classwork portion of the lesson.

Many lessons move through each activity only once, in sequence, but some lessons cycle through the second and third activities twice or even three times.

The Japanese Pattern

Japanese lessons often follow a sequence of five activities.

- *Reviewing the previous lesson.* The review is conducted by a brief teacher lecture, or by the teacher's leading a discussion, or by the students' reciting the main points. Frequently, the day's lesson builds directly on the previous day's lesson, perhaps by using the methods that were developed on the previous day to solve the current day's problem. In the lesson from Chapter 3, Mr. Yoshida asked students to present again, in more detail, the previous day's methods with the expectation that the students would put these methods to use in the current day's lesson.
- *Presenting the problem for the day.* Usually, there is one key problem that sets the stage for most of the work during the lesson.
- *Students working individually or in groups.* This almost always follows the presentation of the problem and lasts anywhere from one to twenty minutes, often five to ten minutes. Students rarely work in small groups to solve problems until they have worked first by themselves.
- *Discussing solution methods.* After the students have worked on the problem, one or more solution methods are presented and discussed. Often, the teacher asks one or more students to share what they have found. Teachers often select students to share (rather than taking volunteers) based on the methods they have seen students develop as they circulated around the room. Sometimes, teachers themselves present methods they have seen students using or new methods they want students to learn. When students present methods, the teacher often summarizes and elaborates.

- *Highlighting and summarizing the major points.* Usually at the end of the lesson, and sometimes during the lesson, the teacher presents a brief lecture on the main point(s) of the lesson. Mr. Yoshida summarized the main point after the opening ten-minute review and again very briefly at the end of the lesson.

Activities two through five can be cycled through several times in one lesson, but usually not more than twice. When a second problem is presented, it often is much like the first, and students are expected to practice the method(s) presented for solving the first problem.

The U.S. Pattern

The pattern of eighth-grade mathematics instruction in the United States shares some elements with the German pattern, but it devotes more time to practicing definitions and procedures and less time to developing the technical details and rationale of procedures. Four activities characterize U.S. lessons.

- *Reviewing previous material.* The lesson begins by checking homework or engaging in a warm-up activity. Mr. Jones conducted a warm-up activity and then checked homework, an opening that is quite common.
- *Demonstrating how to solve problems for the day.* After homework is checked, the teacher introduces new material, or reviews previous material, by presenting a few sample problems and demonstrating how to solve them. Often the teacher engages the students in a step-by-step demonstration by asking short-answer questions along the way.
- *Practicing.* Seatwork is assigned, and students are asked to

complete problems similar to those for which the solution method was demonstrated. Seatwork usually is done individually, although sometimes students work in small groups to compare answers and help one another.

- *Correcting seatwork and assigning homework.* Near the end of the lesson, some of the seatwork problems are checked and, occasionally, some additional problems are worked out together. Homework, with more practice problems, is then assigned. Usually, some time is allowed during the lesson for students to begin the homework.

Versions of activities two through four can be cycled through several times. In Mr. Jones's class, there were several demonstrations of definitions and procedures sandwiched around seatwork and checking homework and seatwork.

Comparing the Lesson Patterns

The three patterns share some basic features: the class reviewing previous material, the teacher presenting problems for the day, and students solving problems at their desks. Apparently, there is some international agreement about the importance of these activities. On closer inspection, however, it becomes clear that these activities play different roles. For example, presenting a problem in Germany sets the stage for a rather long development of a solution procedure, a whole-class activity, guided by the teacher. In Japan, presenting a problem sets the stage for students to work, individually or in groups, on developing solution procedures. In the United States, presenting a problem is the context for demonstrating a procedure and sets the stage for students practicing the procedure. The fact that similar lesson activities can function differently is not surprising, because the activities are embedded in different systems.

There also are differences in the core activities of lessons. For example, at the heart of the German pattern is an activity in which the teacher leads the students through the development of a mathematical procedure. This is not found in either the American or the Japanese pattern. As another example, the Japanese pattern includes an activity in which the teacher summarizes the major point of the lesson. This can be done quite quickly and with little fanfare, but it seems to be a stable part of the lesson design. Taken together, the differences in kinds of activities and in the roles that similar activities can play within the different systems generate large differences across systems of teaching in different cultures.

The Origins of Lesson Patterns

Many people are not surprised to learn that Japanese lessons can be described by a simple, common pattern. After all, Japan is a country with a relatively homogeneous population and a highly centralized education system. Japanese teachers might be expected to teach in similar ways. But the United States seems to be a different case. How is it possible, in a country as diverse and decentralized as our own, to find a national pattern that can characterize teaching? Could a single method of teaching really have developed in this country? This possibility is not as far-fetched as it sounds, especially to those who study education. In fact, the American pattern we have described is consistent with a general method of teaching that has been prevalent in the United States for some time, not only in mathematics and not only in the eighth grade.[3]

The most compelling question is: "Where do these patterns come from, and what accounts for their apparent stability over time?" Of course, patterns that we observe in the classroom come from teachers' heads; it is teachers, after all, who plan and implement the lessons we observe. Indeed, the national patterns of teaching that we have observed must arise out of a knowledge base that is widely shared by teachers within each culture. But where does this shared knowledge come from? One possibility is that it is imparted to teachers in teacher-training programs. Another possibility is that the knowledge is cultural, passed on from generation to generation through human interactions. We contend, as do other educational researchers, that although teachers learn some things about teaching from their formal training, mostly they learn from simple cultural participation.[4] After all, teachers spend at least thirteen years in classrooms, as students, before they even enter a teacher-preparation program. We will explore this idea further in the next chapter.

CHAPTER 6

Teaching Is
a Cultural Activity

F OR MANY PEOPLE, family dinners are everyday events. They participate in these events without realizing all the aspects that are taken for granted. Everyone comes to the table and begins eating at about the same time. Menus are not distributed. Instead, the food is brought to the table in serving dishes and everyone eats the same things. The food is then parceled out by passing the serving dishes around the table, with everyone dishing up his or her own portion. Adults often help children with this task. Conversation usually is open, with no set agenda. Comments from everyone are welcome, with children and adults participating as conversational partners.

Family dinner is a *cultural* activity. Cultural activities are represented in cultural scripts, generalized knowledge about an event that resides in the heads of participants. These scripts guide behavior and also tell participants what to expect. Within a culture, these scripts are widely shared, and therefore they are hard to see. Family dinner is such a familiar activity that it sounds strange to point out all its customary features. We rarely think about how it might be different from what it is. On the other hand, we certainly would notice if a feature were violated; we'd be surprised, for example, to be offered a menu at a family dinner, or to be presented with a check at the end of the meal.

Cultural scripts are learned implicitly, through observation and participation, and not by deliberate study. This differentiates cultural activities from other activities. Take, for example, the activity of learning to use a computer. For older Americans, learning to use the computer is usually not a cultural activity. We learned to use the computer by consciously working on our skills—by reading manuals, taking notes, getting help from experts, and practicing. Using computers is an interesting example because it is rapidly becoming a cultural activity. Children, for example, learn naturally, by hanging around their older siblings. But there still are those for whom it has the distinctly noncultural traits of intentionally, deliberately, and self-consciously working through the activity.

Teaching, in our view, is a cultural activity.[1] It is more like participating in family dinners than like learning to use the computer. This might be surprising, because teaching is rarely thought of in this way. As we noted earlier, some people think that teaching is an innate skill, something you are born with. Others think that teachers learn to teach by enrolling in college teacher-training programs. We believe that neither is the best description. Teaching, like other cultural activities, is learned through informal participation over long periods of time. It is something one learns to do more by growing up in a culture than by studying it formally.

Although most people have not studied to be teachers, most people have been students. People within a culture share a mental picture of what teaching is like. We call this mental picture a *script*. The script is, in fact, a mental version of the teaching patterns we identified in Chapter 5. The difference is that the patterns were observable in the videotapes; scripts are mental models of these patterns. We believe that the scripts provide an explanation for why the lessons within a country followed distinctive patterns: the lessons were designed and taught by teachers who share the same scripts.

It is not hard to see where the scripts come from or why they are widely shared. A cultural script for teaching begins forming early, sometimes even before children get to school. Playing school is a favorite preschool game. As children move through twelve years and more of school, they form scripts for teaching. All of us probably could enter a classroom tomorrow and act like a teacher, because we all share this cultural script. In fact, one of the reasons classrooms run as smoothly as they do is that students and teachers have the same script in their heads: they know what to expect and what roles to play.

Implications of Teaching as a Cultural Activity

We have already made the point that teaching is a complex system, and we have pointed out some implications of this fact. To say that teaching is a cultural activity reveals an additional truth about teaching: Cultural activities, such as teaching, are not invented full-blown but rather evolve over long periods of time in ways that are consistent with the stable web of beliefs and assumptions that are part of the culture. The scripts for teaching in each country appear to rest on a relatively small and tacit set of core beliefs about the nature of the subject, about how students learn, and about the role that a teacher should play in the classroom.[2] These beliefs, often implicit, serve to maintain the stability of cultural systems over time. Just as we have pointed out that features of teaching need to be understood in terms of the underlying systems in which they are embedded, so, too, these systems of teaching, because they are cultural, must be understood in relation to the cultural beliefs and assumptions that surround them.

Let's return to the example of the chalkboard versus the overhead projector. Recall that many teachers in the United States have replaced the chalkboard with the overhead projector, whereas Japanese teachers have not. In Chapter 5 we explained this difference in terms of the different instructional systems in which the visual aids are used. In U.S. classrooms visual aids function to guide and control students' attention. Seen in this light, the overhead projector is preferred because it gives teachers even more control over what students are attending to. Within the Japanese system of teaching, visual aids serve a different function. They are not used to control attention but to provide a cumulative record of the lesson's activities and their results. Japanese teachers do not use the overhead projector because it is not possible to fit the cumulative record on an overhead transparency.

To dig deeper we must ask why Japanese teachers want a cumulative record of the lesson to be available to students and why U.S. teachers want to control students' attention. To answer these questions we need to situate these two systems of teaching in the context of cultural beliefs about how students learn and about the role the teacher can play in this process.

Cultural Beliefs About Teaching and Learning: Japan and the United States

As we pursue deeper comparisons of teaching, we focus on Japan and the United States because this comparison is the most dramatic, and therefore illustrates well the role that beliefs play in generating and maintaining cultural scripts for teaching.

Nature of Mathematics

The typical U.S. lesson is consistent with the belief that school mathematics is a set of procedures. Although teachers might understand that other things must be added to these procedures to get the complete definition of mathematics, many *behave* as if mathematics is a subject whose use for students, in the end, is as a set of procedures for solving problems.

In our study, teachers were asked what "main thing" they wanted students to learn from the lesson. Sixty-one percent of U.S. teachers described *skills* they wanted their students to learn. They wanted the students to be able to perform a procedure, solve a particular kind of problem, and so on.

Many U.S. teachers also seem to believe that learning terms and practicing skills is not very exciting. We have watched them trying to jazz up the lesson and increase students' interest in nonmathematical ways: by being entertaining, by interrupting the lesson to talk about other things (last night's local rock concert, for example), or by setting the mathematics problem in a real-life or intriguing context—for example, measuring the circumference of a basketball. Teachers act as if student interest will be generated only by diversions outside of mathematics.

Japanese lessons appear to be generated by different beliefs about the subject. Teachers act as if mathematics is a set of relationships between concepts, facts, and procedures. These relationships are revealed by developing solution methods to problems, studying the methods, working toward increasingly efficient methods, and talking explicitly about the relationships of interest.

On the same questionnaire, 73 percent of Japanese teachers

said that the main thing they wanted their students to learn from the lesson was to think about things in a new way, such as to see new relationships between mathematical ideas.

Japanese teachers also act as if mathematics is inherently interesting and students will be interested in exploring it by developing new methods for solving problems. They seem less concerned about motivating the topics in nonmathematical ways.

Nature of Learning

If one believes that mathematics is mostly a set of procedures and the goal is to help students become proficient executors of the procedures, as many U.S. teachers seem to, then it would be understandable to believe that mathematics is learned best by mastering the material incrementally, piece by piece. This view of skill learning has a long history in the United States.[3] Learning procedures occurs by practicing them many times, with later exercises being slightly more difficult than earlier ones. Practice should be relatively error-free, with high levels of success at each point. Confusion and frustration, in this traditional American view, should be minimized; they are signs that earlier material was not mastered. The more exercises, the more smoothly learning will proceed.

Suppose students are studying how to add and subtract fractions with unlike denominators, such as $2/3 + 4/7$. The U.S. beliefs about learning described above would dictate that students should first master adding fractions with like denominators, such as $1/5 + 2/5$, then be shown how to add simple fractions with unlike denominators, such as $1/2 + 1/4$, being warned about the common error of adding the denominators (to minimize this error), and later practice more difficult problems, such as $2/3 + 4/7$.

Japanese teachers appear to hold a different set of beliefs

about learning and probably would plan a different kind of lesson for adding fractions. One can infer that Japanese teachers believe students learn best by first struggling to solve mathematics problems, then participating in discussions about how to solve them, and then hearing about the pros and cons of different methods and the relationships between them. Frustration and confusion are taken to be a natural part of the process, because each person must struggle with a situation or problem first in order to make sense of the information he or she hears later. Constructing connections between methods and problems is thought to require time to explore and invent, to make mistakes, to reflect, and to receive the needed information at an appropriate time.[4]

What kind of lesson on adding and subtracting fractions with unlike denominators would these beliefs generate? A teacher's manual in a popular Japanese textbook series gives us a clue.[5] It alerts teachers that the error students are most likely to make is to add the denominators. Students will learn to understand the process more fully, says the manual, if they are allowed to make this mistake and then examine the consequences. Some suggestions are given for how to help students reflect on the inconsistencies they will encounter if they add, for example, $\frac{1}{2}$ and $\frac{1}{4}$, and get $\frac{2}{6}$. Teachers are to begin the lesson with a problem like this and then compare the different methods for solution that students develop. Obviously, struggling and making mistakes and then seeing why they are mistakes are believed to be essential parts of the learning process in Japan.

Role of the Teacher

Given the differences between the United States and Japan in the apparent beliefs about the subject and learning, it is not surprising that marked differences can be inferred regarding beliefs about the role of the teacher. U.S. teachers appear to feel responsible for shaping the task into pieces that are manageable for most students, providing all the information needed to complete the task and assigning plenty of practice. Providing sufficient information means, in many cases, demonstrating how to complete a task just like those assigned for practice. Teachers act as if confusion and frustration are signs that they have not done their job. When they notice confusion, they quickly assist students by providing whatever information it takes to get the students back on track.

We saw the following sequence of events over and over. Teachers assign students seatwork problems and circulate around the room, tutoring and monitoring students' progress. Several students ask, in quick succession, about the same problem. Teachers interrupt the class and say, for example, "Number twenty-three may be a little confusing. Remember to put all the x-terms on one side of the equation and all the y-terms on the other, and then solve for y. That should give the answer." In Mr. Jones's lesson (presented in Chapter 3), these problems were numbers 37 and 38, and as soon as he sensed that the students had reached them during their seatwork and were struggling, he stepped in to show the solutions. Teachers in the United States try hard to reduce confusion by presenting full information about how to solve problems.

U.S. teachers also take responsibility for keeping students engaged and attending. Given their beliefs about the nature of mathematics and how it is learned, moment-by-moment attention is crucial. If students are watching the teacher demonstrate a procedure, they need to attend to each step. If their attention wanders, they will be lost when they try to execute the procedure on their own. Now we have a deeper explanation for the frequent use of the overhead projector by U.S.

teachers. The projector's capability of focusing attention fits well with the teachers' beliefs about teaching mathematics.

In addition to the use of overhead projectors, U.S. teachers use a variety of other techniques to hold students' attention. They pump up students' interest by increasing the pace of the activities, by praising students for their work and behavior, by the cuteness or real-lifeness of tasks, and by their own power of persuasion through their enthusiasm, humor, and "coolness."

Japanese teachers apparently believe they are responsible for different aspects of classroom activity. They often choose a challenging problem to begin the lesson, and they help students understand and represent the problem so they can begin working on a solution. While students are working, the teachers monitor their solution methods so they can organize the follow-up discussion when students share solutions. They also encourage students to keep struggling in the face of difficulty, sometimes offering hints to support students' progress. Rarely would teachers show students how to solve the problem midway through the lesson.

Japanese teachers lead class discussions, asking questions about the solution methods presented, pointing out important features of students' methods, and presenting methods themselves. Because they seem to believe that learning mathematics means constructing relationships between facts, procedures, and ideas, they try to create a visual record of these different methods as the lesson proceeds. Apparently, it is not as important for students to attend at each moment of the lesson as it is for them to be able to go back and think again about earlier events, and to see connections between the different parts of the lesson. Now we understand why Japanese teachers prefer the chalkboard to the overhead projector. Indeed, now we see, in a deeper way, why they cannot use the projector.

Individual Differences

As a consequence of their implicit beliefs about the subject, learning, and the teacher's role, all teachers appear to hold a set of beliefs about individual differences among students. Many U.S. teachers believe that individual differences are an obstacle to effective teaching.[6] Meeting each student's needs means, ideally, diagnosing each student's level of performance and providing different instruction for different levels. This is not easy to do in a large class. As the range of differences increases, the difficulties of teaching increase. In simple terms, this is an obvious reason for tracking students into separate classes by ability or past performance. It is also the reason for reform efforts directed toward reducing class size. This belief says that the tutoring situation is best, academically, because instruction can be tailored specifically for each student or small group of students.

Japanese teachers view individual differences as a natural characteristic of a *group*. They view differences in the mathematics class as a resource for both students and teachers.[7] Individual differences are beneficial for the class because they produce a range of ideas and solution methods that provide the material for students' discussion and reflection. The variety of alternative methods allows students to compare them and construct connections among them. It is believed that all students benefit from the variety of ideas generated by their peers. In addition, tailoring instruction to specific students is seen as unfairly limiting and as prejudging what students are capable of learning; all students should have the opportunity to learn the same material.

For the Japanese teacher, the differences within a group are beneficial because they allow a teacher to plan a lesson more completely. Japanese teachers plan lessons by using the information that they and other teachers have previously recorded about students' likely responses to particular problems and questions. If the group is sufficiently large, they can be quite sure that these same responses will be given by these students. They can then plan the nature of the discussion that is likely to occur. The range of responses also provides the vehicle teachers use to meet the needs of different students. It is expected that different students will understand different methods and will think about the material at different levels of sophistication. Not all students will be prepared to learn the same things from each lesson, and the different methods that are shared allow each student to learn some things.

Sanctity of the Lesson

Another set of beliefs pertains to the significance of the classroom lesson. Lessons, of course, are the most common form of teaching. Classroom teaching, as it is known around the world, plays out through daily lessons. Students' lives in most schools are organized around the series of 45- to 60-minute periods that they move through in the course of a day. But different beliefs about teaching lead to treating lessons in quite different ways.

In Japan, classroom lessons hold a privileged place in the activities of the school. It would be exaggerating only a little to say they are sacred. They are treated much as we treat lectures in university courses or religious services in church. A great deal of attention is given to their development.[8] They are planned as complete experiences—as stories with a beginning, a middle, and an end. Their meaning is found in the connections between the parts. If you stay for only the beginning, or leave before the end, you miss the point. If lessons like this are going to succeed, they must be coherent. The pieces must relate to one another in clear ways. And they must flow along, free from interruptions and unrelated activities. It is clear why Japanese lessons we videotaped were never interrupted from the outside, not by P.A. announcements, not by lunch-count monitors, not by anyone.

It is quite easy to see how Japanese beliefs about mathematics, learning, and the role of the teacher lead to treating lessons in this way. In this belief system, mathematics is made up of relationships between ideas, facts, and procedures. To understand these relationships, students must analyze mathematical problems and different methods that can be used to solve them. They must struggle with problems first in order to make sense of later discussions about how to solve them and to understand the summary comments made by the teacher. So the lesson must tell a tightly connected, coherent story; the teacher must build a visible record of the pieces as they unfold so connections can be drawn between them; and the lesson cannot be sidetracked or broken by interruptions.

In the United States, lessons are treated differently. This is not surprising given the different beliefs about mathematics, learning, and the teacher. The activities within a lesson are more modular, with fewer connections between them. Practice time might be devoted to the procedures demonstrated on the current day, on the previous day, or during the previous week. Because learning procedures is believed to depend largely on practicing them, temporary interruptions, like outside intrusions or unrelated activities, do not ruin the lesson. They might be annoying, but they just reduce the number of practice exercises for that day. It might not be surprising, then, that we found that almost one-third of the U.S. lessons were interrupted in some way.

Changing Cultural Activities

Cultural activities are highly stable over time, and they are not easily changed. This is true for two reasons. First, cultural activities are systems, and systems—especially complex ones, such as teaching—can be very difficult to change. The second reason is that cultural activities are embedded in a wider culture, often in ways not readily apparent to members of the culture. If we want to improve teaching, both its systemic and its cultural aspects must be recognized and addressed.

Teaching systems, like other complex systems, are composed of elements that interact and reinforce one another; the whole is greater than the sum of the parts. An immediate implication of this fact is that it will be difficult, if not impossible, to improve teaching by changing individual elements or features. In a system, all the features reinforce each other. If one feature is changed, the system will rush to "repair the damage," perhaps by modifying the new feature so it functions the way the old one did. If all teachers in the United States started using the chalkboard rather than the overhead projector, teaching would not change much. The chalkboard simply would be used to fill the visual-aids slot in their system and therefore would be used just as the overhead projector was— to catch and hold students' attention.

This point is missed in many popular attempts to reform teaching in the United States. These reforms start with indicators, like the ones we presented in Chapter 4, and try to improve teaching by influencing the level of the indicator. For example, having found that Japanese and German students encounter more advanced mathematics, reformers might propose that we present more challenging content in our schools. Or because

Japanese teachers switch back and forth between classwork and seatwork more often than American teachers do, they might propose lessons with shorter classwork and seatwork segments. German and Japanese students do proofs, so perhaps we should include proofs in our lessons. Educational reforms in this country often have been driven by an effort to change our performance on quantifiable indicators like these.[9]

But because teaching is a complex system, these attempts to change it generally don't work. It has now been documented in several studies that teachers asked to change features of their teaching often modify the features to fit within their pre-existing system instead of changing the system itself. The system assimilates individual changes and swallows them up. Thus, although surface features appear to change, the fundamental nature of the instruction does not. When this happens, anticipated improvements in student learning fail to materialize and everyone wonders why.[10]

A well-known example comes from the New Math reforms of the 1960s. A major thrust of these reforms was changing the textbooks.[11] Because most mathematics teachers rely quite heavily on the textbook,[12] one might think that changing the textbook would change teaching. In 1975, after the changes had had time to take effect, the National Advisory Committee on Mathematical Education commissioned a study of school mathematics instruction. The study concluded that in elementary schools, "Teachers are essentially teaching the same way they were taught in school. Almost none of the concepts, methods, or big ideas of modern mathematics have appeared."[13] Even textbooks can get swamped by the system.

A more recent and personal illustration of the stability of systems of teaching occurred when one of us was working with a group of American teachers studying videotapes of Japanese mathematics instruction. After viewing the Japanese lessons, a fourth-grade teacher decided to shift from his traditional approach to a more problem-solving approach such as we had seen on the videotapes. Instead of asking short-answer questions as he regularly did, he began his next lesson by presenting a problem and asking students to spend ten minutes working on a solution. Although the teacher changed his behavior to correspond with the actions of the teacher in the videotape, the students, not having seen the video or reflected upon their own participation, failed to respond as the students on the tape did. They played their traditional roles. They waited to be shown how to solve the problem. The lesson did not succeed. The students are part of the system.

Systems of teaching are much more than the things the teacher does. They include the physical setting of the classroom; the goals of the teacher; the materials, including textbooks and district or state objectives; the roles played by the students; the way the school day is scheduled; and other factors that influence how teachers teach. Changing any one of these individual features is unlikely to have the intended effect.

Trying to improve teaching by changing individual features usually makes little difference, positive or negative. But it can backfire and leave things worse than before.[14] When one or two features are changed, and the system tries to run as before, it can operate in a disabled state. Geoffrey Saxe and his colleagues at UCLA found that when elementary school teachers were asked to teach fractions by implementing an innovative curriculum, some did so with higher student achievement than a comparison traditional program and some did so with lower student achievement.[15] The difference was that the successful teachers were provided with information and assistance by the project staff that, in our words, helped them improve their *system*. The less-successful teachers did not receive such assistance and tried to operate their conventional system with the new curriculum. This was not a good fit and did not promote students' learning. The point here is that trying to improve by changing individual features is not just ineffective; it is down-right risky.

Bombarding teachers with waves of ineffective reforms can have another downside: Teachers can grow weary. They are asked over and over to change the way they do x, y, or z. Even when they try to accommodate the reformers and adopt a new feature or two, nothing much happens. They do not notice much improvement in students' learning. Although it might feel to teachers that they are changing, the basic system is running essentially as it did before. Always changing, and yet staying the same, is a discouraging state of affairs. It can lead to a defeatist kind of cynicism. "Not another reform," says the veteran teacher; "I'll just wait this one out." Quick fixes that focus on changing individual features leave behind a skeptical teaching corps.

The fact that teaching is cultural only further complicates and impedes efforts to change it. The widely shared cultural beliefs and expectations that underlie teaching are so fully integrated into teachers' worldviews that they fail to see them as mutable. The more widely shared a belief is, the less likely it is to be questioned—or even noticed. This tends to natural-ize the most common aspects of teaching to the point that teachers fail to see alternatives to what they are doing in the classroom, thinking, "This is just the way things are." Even if someone wanted to change, things that seem this natural are perceived as unchangeable. It is no wonder that the way we teach has not changed much for many years.

Is it impossible to change? We don't think so. But we must be sure that our efforts to improve are appropriate for changing *cultural* activities. If teaching were a noncultural activity, we could try to improve it simply by providing better information in teachers' manuals, or asking experts to demonstrate better techniques, or distributing written recommendations on more effective teaching methods. Note that this is exactly what we have been doing. We have been acting as if teaching is a noncultural activity.

If we took seriously the notion that teaching is a cultural activity, we would begin the improvement process by becoming more aware of the cultural scripts teachers are using. This requires comparing scripts, seeing that other scripts are possible, and noticing things about our own scripts that we had never seen before. Becoming more aware of the scripts we use helps us see that they come from choices we make. The choices might be understandable, but still they are choices, and once we are aware of them, other choices can be made.

Improving cultural scripts for teaching is a dramatically different approach from improving the skills of individual teachers, but it is the approach called for if teaching is a cultural activity. No matter how good teachers are, they will be only as effective as the script they are using. To improve teaching over the long run, we must improve the script.

Of course, knowing what must be done and actually doing it are two very different things, especially when it comes to complex, culturally embedded activities. Once again, we can learn something important by contrasting our own situation with that of others. In the next chapter, we look at how Japan has dealt with the challenge of improving teaching.

CHAPTER 7

Beyond Reform:
Japan's Approach
to the Improvement
of Classroom Teaching

W E HAVE LEARNED that teaching is not a simple skill but rather a complex cultural activity that is highly determined by beliefs and habits that work partly outside the realm of consciousness. That teaching is largely a cultural activity helps to explain why, in the face of constant reform, so little has actually changed inside U.S. classrooms. The cultural nature of teaching might also help to explain why teaching per se has rarely been the direct focus of efforts to reform education. Teaching is so constant within our own culture that we fail even to imagine how it might be changed, much less believe that it should be changed.

On the other hand, our cross-cultural investigations have also revealed a different, yet equally important, fact about teaching: Although highly constant within a culture, variations in teaching methods across cultures are significant. This means that teaching might be an even more important influence on student learning than some studies have suggested. When studies are conducted within cultures, they might underestimate the effects of teaching because they probably are comparing methods that do not differ greatly from one another. The substantive differences in teaching that we see across cultures suggests that very different ways of teaching can be designed and implemented, and that these substantive changes might have large effects on students' learning. This bolsters our belief that efforts to directly improve classroom processes can lead to significant gains in students' learning.

In this chapter we briefly discuss the way reformers have sought to improve teaching in the United States, and we use the TIMSS videos to assess how successful these efforts have been. Then we briefly examine Japan's very different approach to the improvement of classroom teaching. Japan's record of high student achievement, together with its contrasting methods of teaching, entreats us to examine how Japan goes about improving its practice.

Reform in the United States: Evidence from the Classroom

Although most popular U.S. reform efforts have avoided a direct focus on teaching, there are some notable exceptions.[1] One of these has been in the domain of mathematics, where the National Council of Teachers of Mathematics (NCTM) has made a strong effort to improve classroom mathematics teaching. The NCTM believes that teaching is of major importance in trying to explain students' learning of mathematics and has led a far-reaching campaign to move teachers in the direction of more effective practices.

The strategy employed by NCTM in this crusade exemplifies a common approach to reform in the United States. Experts are convened to review the research and experience of the profession and to formulate recommendations for change. These recommendations then are put in written documents that are widely disseminated. One of these documents, the NCTM's *Professional Standards for Teaching Mathematics,* is quite explicit in its vision of how teaching needs to change in order to raise the level of students' learning.[2] The changes envisioned by NCTM are substantial.

Investigating the success of these NCTM efforts, and of similar efforts, was a major goal of the TIMSS video study. The findings are quite interesting. First of all, the good news: U.S. teachers appear to be highly aware of reforms advocated by NCTM and other organizations. We asked all of the video-taped teachers, on a questionnaire, to rate their awareness of current ideas regarding the best ways to teach mathematics. Almost all (95 percent) of the U.S. teachers sampled said they were "somewhat aware" or "very aware" of such ideas, with most claiming to have read documents published by NCTM or similar documents (such as California's Mathematics Framework). Not only are teachers aware of the reforms, the majority claimed to be implementing the reforms in their classrooms. When asked whether or not they implement reforms in their classrooms, and whether or not we would find evidence of such in the videotape we collected from their rooms, 70 percent of U.S. teachers we asked responded in the affirmative. The teachers even pointed us to specific places in the videos where we could see examples of their implementation of reform.

But this is where the good news ends. When we looked at the videos, we found little evidence of reform, at least as intended by those who had proposed the reforms. Looking at the situation as a whole, one might even argue that Japanese lessons better exemplify current U.S. reform ideas than do U.S. lessons. Japanese lessons, for example, emphasized student thinking and problem solving, multiple solution methods, and the kinds of discourse described in U.S. reform documents to a greater extent than U.S. lessons did. And this is not the worst of it. When we examined the places in the video that teachers referred to as examples of reform, we saw a disturbing confirmation of the suspicion we voiced in Chapter 6—that reform teaching, as interpreted by some teachers, might actually be worse than what they were doing previously in their classrooms.

One teacher, for example, pointed to her use of calculators as an instance of reform in her classroom. True, NCTM recommends that calculators be introduced early in the curriculum, because, among other reasons, they can save computing time so students can focus their attention on problem solving and conceptual understanding. But this was not the way calculators were being used in this particular teacher's classroom. Midway through the solution of a simple problem, the class needed the answer to the problem 1 – 4. "Take out your calculators," the teacher said. "Now, follow along with me. Push the one. Push the minus sign. Push the four. Now push the equals sign. What do you get?" The calculator, in this case, was a diversion, and accomplished little on behalf of students' mathematical understanding.

Examples like this one point to a problem in the U.S. approach to reform. Teachers can misinterpret reform and change surface features—for example, they include more group work; use more manipulatives, calculators, and real-world problem scenarios; or include writing in the lesson—but fail to alter their basic approach to teaching mathematics.

Albert Shanker, the late leader of the American Federation of Teachers, clearly anticipated this possibility. He often told a story of a trip he had made years earlier with his wife, Eadie. They were touring a housing project, a section that housed recently arrived Jews from African and Arabic countries. Shanker told the story this way:

> As we were touring this housing project, we were told that most of these people had lived in tents or in very primitive housing and that most of them had not eaten on tables. There was this concerted effort to convince them to use tables. As we went through the development, our guides said, "Let's visit one of these families; let's take a look at an apartment." And they knocked at a door and said, "We have Mr. and Mrs. Shanker here from New York; can they come in?" We walked in, and there was a family from Yemen, and they were eating from the table. But the table was upside down with the top on the floor and the legs standing up.[3]

Shanker understood that teaching, like eating, is a cultural activity and that it is governed by powerful forces that function largely outside of conscious awareness, forces that change slowly over time—if they change at all. Like the Yemeni immigrants, teachers can misinterpret the intentions of reformers, engaging in practices that verge on the bizarre. As we noted earlier, reform documents that focus teachers' attention on features of "good teaching" in the absence of supporting contexts might actually divert attention away from the more important goals of student learning. They may inadvertently cause teachers to substitute the means for the ends—to define success in terms of specific features or activities instead of long-term improvements in learning. To the extent that this occurs, the best-laid plans of reformers will backfire. Far from being benign or simply ignored, reform recommendations might even worsen the quality of instruction. We are not the only researchers to document this phenomenon.[4] But the TIMSS videotapes reveal that the problem is national in scope.

At first glance, this misapplication of reform seems quite discouraging: Given the energy that we as a nation have invested in reform, it is shocking to realize how little penetration there has been into the classroom. But on the other hand, given the cultural, systemic nature of teaching described earlier in this book, it would be surprising if reform *were* successful—at least the type of reform that has been most widely practiced in the United States. Features of teaching recommended in documents such as the NCTM standards are easily misinterpreted, lacking reference to either the system of teaching in which they are embedded or the wider cultural beliefs that support them. This helps to explain how teachers could be aware of the NCTM's reform recommendations, and even think they were implementing them in the videotaped lesson, when, in fact, they often were aligning their teaching with the recommendations in only superficial ways.

Disseminating models of effective teaching through static documents might work if teaching were a *noncultural* activity. If teachers learned to teach by studying books and memorizing techniques, written recommendations might have their intended effect. But everything we have learned indicates that teaching is a cultural activity, and consequently the writing and dissemination of reform documents is an unrealistic way to improve education.

What are the alternatives? We were drawn initially to Japan's system of improvement as one possibility, because of Japanese students' high levels of achievement and because Japanese teaching methods provide such a clear contrast to our own. But we found another reason to examine Japan's system of improvement more closely: It is built on the idea that teaching is a complex, cultural activity. Just as we saw the U.S. method of teaching in a new way by comparing it with methods in other countries, so too can we use other systems of improvement to envision the possibilities in our own country more clearly.

Lesson Study: Japan's Alternative to Reform

Despite years of reform, research suggests that classroom teaching has changed little in the United States. In Japan, by contrast, teaching practices appear to have changed markedly over the past fifty years.[5] What accounts for this difference? Japan, too, has sought to reform its educational practices.[6] But the assumptions about how reform must work, and the mechanisms established to enact reform, are quite distinct from those in the United States. Whereas U.S. educators have sought major changes over relatively short time periods—indeed, the very word *reform* connotes sudden and wholesale change—Japanese educators have instituted a system that leads to gradual, incremental improvements in teaching over time. The system includes clear learning goals for students, a shared curriculum, the support of administrators, and the hard work of teachers striving to make gradual improvements in their practice.

Japan has given teachers themselves primary responsibility

for the improvement of classroom practice. *Kounaikenshuu* is the word used to describe the continuous process of school-based professional development that Japanese teachers engage in once they begin their teaching careers. In the United States, teachers are assumed to be competent once they have completed their teacher-training programs. Japan makes no such assumption. Participation in school-based professional development groups is considered part of the teacher's job in Japan. These groups play a dual role: not only do they provide a context in which teachers are mentored and trained, they also provide a laboratory for the development and testing of new teaching techniques.

Virtually every elementary and middle school in Japan is engaged in *kounaikenshuu*.[7] Run by teachers, *kounaikenshuu* consists of a diverse set of activities that together constitute a comprehensive process of school improvement. Teachers work together in grade-level groups, in subject-matter groups (for example, math or language arts), and in special committees (the technology committee, for example). The activities of these various groups are coordinated by a school-improvement plan that sets the goals and focus for each year's efforts. A significant percentage of teachers also engage in district-wide groups that meet in the evenings, generally on a monthly basis. Teachers spend a considerable amount of time each month on *kounaikenshuu*.[8]

Lesson Study

One of the most common components of *kounaikenshuu* is lesson study (*jugyou kenkyuu*). In lesson study, groups of teachers meet regularly over long periods of time (ranging from several months to a year) to work on the design, implementation, testing, and improvement of one or several "research lessons" (*kenkyuu jugyou*). By all indications, lesson study is extremely popular and highly valued by Japanese teachers, especially at the elementary school level. It is the linchpin of the improvement process. One elementary school teacher interviewed by Catherine Lewis and Ineko Tsuchida, scholars of Japanese education, remarked, "You won't find a school without research lessons."[9]

The premise behind lesson study is simple: If you want to improve teaching, the most effective place to do so is in the context of a classroom lesson. If you start with lessons, the problem of how to apply research findings in the classroom disappears. The improvements are devised within the classroom in the first place. The challenge now becomes that of identifying the kinds of changes that will improve student learning in the classroom and, once the changes are identified, of sharing this knowledge with other teachers who face similar problems, or share similar goals, in the classroom.

Very little has been written in English about the process of lesson study. We base our account on research conducted by Makoto Yoshida, by Catherine Lewis and Ineko Tsuchida, and by N. Ken Shimahara, as well as on informal discussions with teachers and teacher educators throughout Japan.[10] Most of our specific examples will be drawn from the work of Yoshida.

In Tsuta Elementary School, the Hiroshima school studied by Yoshida, the lesson-study process was divided into trimesters. During the first trimester, teachers met first in several school-wide meetings to determine the theme or focus of the year's *kounaikenshuu* efforts. Once a general theme was chosen, teachers continued meeting in grade-level groups to begin developing the goal that would guide their lesson study for the year. Because Tsuta Elementary School was a small school, the teachers divided into three groups: one each for lower, middle, and upper grades. Larger schools might divide into separate groups for each grade level, with a goal of keeping the sizes of the groups at approximately five to seven teachers.

In the second trimester, the teacher groups started developing "research lessons." The group that Yoshida studied focused on first-graders' understanding of subtraction with borrowing. They met weekly, on Thursday afternoons, for approximately three to four hours. The principal and the head teacher of the school generally sat in with the group in an ex officio capacity.

Steps in the Lesson Study Process

Although the form of lesson study varies throughout Japan, we can describe the steps that seem to typify the process.

Step 1: Defining the Problem. Lesson study is, fundamentally, a problem-solving process. The first step, therefore, is to define the problem that will motivate and direct the work of the lesson-study group. The problem can start out as a general one (for example, to awaken students' interest in mathematics) or it can be more specific (for example, to improve students' understanding of how to add fractions with unlike denominators). The group will then shape and focus the problem until it can be addressed by a specific classroom lesson.

Usually the problem teachers choose is one they have identified from their own practice, something that has posed particular challenges for their own students. Sometimes, however, the problem is posed from above, perhaps by educational policymakers seeking teachers' input on problems identified as national priorities. The National Ministry of Education will ask a general question—how can we help students become independent learners, for example—and invite a sample of schools throughout the country to study the question in the context of lesson study and report their findings. At other times, the administrative authorities issue recommendations that teachers are expected to implement. This combination of top-down and bottom-up planning is a unique feature of the educational policy environment in Japan, and it provides a direct connection between classroom teachers and national education officials.

Step 2: Planning the Lesson. Once a learning goal has been chosen, teachers begin meeting to plan the lesson. Although one teacher will ultimately teach the lesson as part of the process, the lesson itself is seen by all involved as a group product. Often the teachers will start their planning by looking at books and articles produced by other teachers who have studied a similar problem. According to one Japanese book on how to prepare a research lesson, the useful research lesson should be designed with a hypothesis in mind: some idea to be tested and worked out within the context of classroom practice.[11] The goal is not only to produce an effective lesson but also to understand why and how the lesson works to promote understanding among students. The initial plan that the group produces is often presented at a schoolwide faculty meeting in order to solicit criticism. Based on such feedback, a revision is produced, ready for implementation. This initial planning process can take as long as several months.

Step 3: Teaching the Lesson. A date is set to teach the lesson. One teacher will teach the lesson, but everyone in the group will participate fully in the preparation. The night before, the group might stay late at school, preparing materials and engaging in a dress rehearsal, complete with role playing. On the day of the lesson, the other teachers in the group leave their classrooms to observe the lesson being taught. (Teachers leave their classrooms without adult supervision.

Two students, appointed to serve as class monitors, are left in charge of the class.) The teachers stand or sit in the back as the lesson begins, but when students are asked to work at their desks, the teacher-observers walk around, observing and taking careful notes on what students are doing as the lesson progresses. Sometimes the lesson is videotaped as well, for later analysis and discussion.

Step 4: Evaluating the Lesson and Reflecting on Its Effect. The group generally stays after school to meet on the day the lesson has been taught. Usually, the teacher who taught the lesson is allowed to speak first, outlining in his or her own view how the lesson worked and what the major problems were. Then other members of the group speak, usually critically, about the parts of the lesson they saw as problematic. The focus is on the lesson, not on the teacher who taught the lesson; the lesson, after all, is a group product, and all members of the group feel responsible for the outcome of their plan. They are, in effect, critiquing themselves. This is important, because it shifts the focus from a personal evaluation to a self-improvement activity.

Step 5: Revising the Lesson. Based on their observations and reflections, teachers in the lesson-study group revise the lesson. They might change the materials, the activities, the problems posed, the questions asked, or all these things. They often will base their changes on specific misunderstandings evidenced by students as the lesson progressed.

Step 6: Teaching the Revised Lesson. Once the revised lesson is ready, the lesson is taught again to a different class. Sometimes it is taught by the same teacher who taught the lesson the first time, but often it is taught by another member of the group. One difference is that this time all members of the school faculty are invited to attend the research lesson. This is quite dramatic in a large school, where there may be more faculty crowded into the classroom than there are students in the class.

Step 7: Evaluating and Reflecting, Again. This time, it is common for all members of the school faculty to participate in a long meeting. Sometimes an outside expert will be invited to attend as well. As before, the teacher who taught the lesson is allowed to speak first, discussing what the group was trying to accomplish, her or his own assessment of how successful the lesson was, and what parts of the lesson still need rethinking. Observers then critique the lesson and suggest changes. Not only is the lesson discussed with respect to what these students learned and understood, but also with respect to more general issues raised by the hypotheses that guided the design of the research lesson. What about teaching and learning, more generally, was learned from the lesson and its implementation?

Step 8: Sharing the Results. All this work has focused on a single lesson. But because Japan is a country with national education goals and curricular guidelines, what this group of teachers has learned will have immediate relevance for other Japanese teachers trying to teach the same concepts at the same grade level. Indeed, the teachers in one lesson-study group see the sharing of their findings as a significant part of the lesson-study process. This sharing can be done in several ways. One is to write a report, and most lesson-study groups do produce a report that tells the story of their group's work. Often these reports are published in book form, even if only for the school's teacher resource room. They are read by the faculty and the principal, and might be forwarded to educational authorities at the prefectural level if judged to be interesting enough. If a university professor happens to have collaborated with the group, the report might be written for a wider audience and published by a commercial publisher.

Another method of sharing the results of a research lesson is to invite teachers from other schools to observe the teaching of the final version of the lesson. The school in Hiroshima that Yoshida observed hosted a "lesson fair" at the end of the school year and invited teachers from schools throughout the region to observe the research lessons they had produced in various subject areas. This is a festive occasion, and it is considered an important part of teachers' professional development. This also is one of the primary ways that teachers can learn about innovations that are being tried at other schools.

What Teachers Talk About:
An Example from Simple Subtraction

We have outlined the general lesson-study process. But what do teachers actually do during their meetings? In this section we again draw on the work of Makoto Yoshida, who spent a year with one lesson-study group in Hiroshima. It is one thing to say that teachers "planned a lesson," quite another to witness the kind of detailed planning that goes on inside these groups. Yoshida brings this across clearly in his description of how a group of lower primary teachers planned the introductory lesson for a first-grade unit on simple subtraction with the minuend larger than ten.

Consistent with the general cultural script for lessons in Japan, the basic flow of the lesson was determined at one of the early meetings of the group. The lesson would start with a problem. Students would work on the problem, then present their various solution methods to the whole class. The teacher would then lead a discussion of the methods students had invented, and conclude the lesson by summarizing the concept that students were intended to understand. But this general flow was only the beginning of what the teachers needed to decide. According to Yoshida, the teachers engaged in detailed discussions of the following topics over the weeks spent planning the lesson:

- The problem with which the lesson would begin, including such details as the exact wording and numbers to be used.
- The materials students would be given to use in trying to solve the problem.
- The anticipated solutions, thoughts, and responses that students might develop as they struggled with the problem.
- The kinds of questions that could be asked to promote student thinking during the lesson, and the kinds of guidance that could be given to students who showed one or another type of misconception in their thinking.
- How to use the space on the chalkboard (Japanese teachers believe that organizing the chalkboard is a key ingredient to organizing students' thinking and understanding).
- How to apportion the fixed time of the lesson—about forty minutes—to different parts of the lesson.
- How to handle individual differences in level of mathematical preparation among the students.
- How to end the lesson—considered a key moment in which students' understanding can be advanced.

During one of the early sessions, the Japanese teachers decided to use this problem at the beginning of the lesson:

_____ (*Student's name*) collected _____ ginkgo leaves. Then he/she drew _____ pictures of his/her family on the leaves, one member on each leaf. How many leaves did not have pictures?

The teachers agreed that it would be good to use one of the students' names in the problem, though they hadn't determined which student. Also still unresolved was the question of what numbers to use in the problem. This question led to a great deal of discussion. Ms. Tsukuda, the teacher who had proposed the problem, began with the following comments, as related by Yoshida:

Not long ago, the Vice-Principal (Ms. Furumoto) showed me several textbooks. All of those textbooks used 12 and 9 (i.e., 12 − 9 =) and 13 and 9. What most of the textbooks said was, they started out by introducing the Subtraction-Addition Method (*Genkahoo*). In the case of 13 − 9, first subtract the nine from ten (10 − 9 = 1), then add what is left over in the 1s position (which is 3) to the number (1 + 3 = 4). I thought if you narrow it down like that (introducing subtraction with borrowing by teaching the Subtraction-Addition Method), it's not very interesting. So on Saturday I suggested using 15 − 8, or 15 − 7. I thought that these are a little harder than 12 − 9 and 13 − 9. Using these numbers will bring out a lot more ideas or ways to solve the problem. But after reading a lot of different books on the subject, because kids can conceptualize in their heads about up to the number 6 at this age, I thought we should go with numbers like 11 − 6.

The teachers agreed that the choice of numbers would influence which strategies the students would try when solving the problem. But they had other concerns as well. For example, one teacher wanted to use 12 − 7, because one of her students, who was a low achiever, happened to have seven family members. Everyone agreed that this was a good idea. They also liked the number 12 because, since none of the students had fewer than three people in their families, subtracting the number of family members from 12 would involve decomposing ten, which was, of course, the point of the lesson. They briefly considered the number 13 instead of 12, but decided against it, as shown in the following dialogue.

Tsukuda: Well, I was thinking. I also thought of using 13 minus 7, but it's really hard to break down 7 into 3 and 4.

Maejima: I see, you mean conceptually.

Tsukuda: Right, conceptually it's easy to break 6 down into 5 and 1, and it's easy to break down 7 into 2 and 5, but it's really hard for first-grade students to break 7 down into 3 and 4.

Once the numbers were agreed on, they wondered how they could make it seem natural that students should start with the number 12. They decided to begin the problem by asking students to select their twelve favorites from among the leaves they had collected. These would be the leaves students would use to work on the problem.

From there the discussion turned to the different strategies that students might be expected to generate. The teachers consulted some of the teachers' manuals and found five common ways of solving simple subtraction problems with borrowing. Each method was labeled with technical terminology that seemed quite familiar to the teachers (though not to the researcher). Ms. Furumoto, who was the vice principal and who had been in the school for only one year, named a particular student who appeared to use only the subtraction-addition method. She said this concerned her, because she found it difficult to move students from this particular method into using more sophisticated methods.

And so the discussion continued, for weeks, touching on all the topics listed above at a level of detail similar to that manifested in this example. This kind of planning is decidedly intellectual in nature; these teachers are thinking deeply about the options available to them and the way the experiences they structure in their classrooms will facilitate students' understanding of mathematics. There is real excitement as this process unfolds, an excitement that is obvious to those who observe the weekly meetings of a lesson-study group.

Reflections on Lesson Study

From the U.S. perspective, it is difficult to believe that a process as narrowly focused as lesson study could really be the driving force behind Japan's educational success. "One year on a single lesson? We could never do that here," mused one of our colleagues. "It would take forever to make any significant improvements in teaching." Yet perhaps that is one of our problems: by being in a hurry and taking the short-term view, we undermine the kinds of gradual long-term improvements that add up to real change.

On reflection, we can identify a number of interesting aspects of lesson study that might contribute to its success. All these aspects appear to be consistent with what we know about changing complex, cultural activities. Yet, significantly, they differ markedly from most opportunities that U.S. teachers have to improve teaching.[12] It is worth examining some of these features.

Lesson Study Is Based on a Long-term Continuous Improvement Model

We have made this point already, but it is worth making again: Lesson study is a process of improvement that is expected to produce small, incremental improvements in teaching over long periods of time. It is emphatically not a reformlike process.

The lesson-study process, as conducted in Japan, thus respects the fact that teaching is a cultural activity. Ronald Gallimore, who has written extensively about these issues, says, "Cultural activities are historically evolved solutions to adaptive challenges. They were constructed over time through collaborative human effort to achieve a stable daily routine. Changes in cultural activity are made slowly, gradually, and are built on existing routines."[13] Because teaching is a cultural activity, it will not change quickly or drastically.

Lesson Study Maintains a Constant Focus on Student Learning

The lesson-study process has an unrelenting focus on student learning. All efforts to improve lessons are evaluated with respect to clearly specified learning goals, and revisions are always justified with respect to student thinking and learning.

Although this feature might seem obvious and trivial, it is not. Reforms in the United States often are tied to particular theories of teaching or to educational fads instead of to specific learning outcomes. Because of this, success often is measured by the degree to which teachers implement recommended practices. Someone is marked as a good teacher because he or she uses cooperative groups or concrete manipulatives, instead of on the basis of his or her students' successful learning.

Lesson Study Focuses on the Direct
Improvement of Teaching in Context

By attending to teaching as it occurs, lesson study respects teaching's complex and systemic nature, and so generates knowledge that is immediately usable. This is in marked distinction to teacher-development programs in the United States, which seek to take knowledge gained in one context (for example, knowledge produced by educational researchers) and translate it into the messy and complex world of the classroom. As useful as educational research might be, it is notoriously difficult to bridge the gap separating researchers and practitioners. Japanese teachers function both as teachers and researchers, making it unnecessary to translate one into the other.

What keeps lesson study relevant to the improvement of classroom teaching is its focus on the *lesson* as the unit to be analyzed and improved. Some might see this focus as trivial: Are there not other, more important, issues that could organize the teachers' inquiry? But in fact, focusing on a particular lesson turns out to be a useful way of simplifying the work of the group while still preserving the complexity that characterizes life in classrooms. The challenge of choosing units for study that retain the important elements of the system one is trying to understand is a classic problem in the research literature, often referred to as the problem of ecological validity. If units that are selected do not have ecological validity, research results often cannot be generalized to actual real-world situations. Lessons, we believe, do have ecological validity. Even a single lesson retains the key complexities—curriculum, student characteristics, materials, and physical environment, among other things—that must be taken into account as we try to improve classroom learning.

The decision to focus on lessons is especially appropriate in Japan. Because Japan has a centralized educational system and a national curriculum, division of the content into lessons is done in a similar way for all teachers of a given grade level and subject. This means that knowledge developed about a specific eighth-grade mathematics lesson or sequence of lessons, for example, is highly sharable with teachers all over Japan who must teach the same lessons. Reports published by lesson-study groups describing their work and its consequences have an instant audience among their colleagues throughout Japan. Many such reports, in fact, can be purchased in neighborhood bookstores.

Lesson Study Is Collaborative

By working in groups to improve instruction, teachers are able to develop a shared language for describing and analyzing classroom teaching, and to teach each other about teaching.

The often-described isolation of U.S. teachers has greatly hindered our discussions about teaching and hence our ability to improve it.[14] U.S. teachers rarely have the opportunity to observe other teachers in action and are rarely observed by other teachers. For whatever reason, teaching in the United States is considered a private, not a public, activity. The consequences of this isolation are severe. Teachers might agree in discussion, for example, that "problem solving" should be a central focus of the mathematics classroom. But in practice, different teachers might have completely different understandings of what "problem solving" entails. The term is the same, but the referent of the term is private and varies from person to person.

All of this might sound abstract and academic, but it is not. Several years ago one of us was invited to a school by the principal to observe one of the school's star math teachers. As we walked into her room, we saw that the third-grade children were in groups, and the teacher was working with one of the groups. "Imagine," said the teacher, "that eight kitten ears were visible over the top of a fence, and a whole bunch of kitten feet were visible below the fence. How many kittens are behind the fence?" Within ten seconds every one of the children's hands shot up. One child, after being called on by the teacher, responded, "Four," to which the teacher responded, "Correct." The process was repeated twelve more times with different problems.

At this point the teacher walked over and said, "Isn't it amazing the kinds of problems these kids are solving?" We were stunned. Why did she call this problem solving? Can a problem that is solvable within ten seconds really be considered a problem? How could she possibly define problem solving with respect to the problem but without reference to the students' level of knowledge and skill relevant to the problem? Clearly, we had no shared understanding of what problem solving is all about.

Another important benefit of the collaborative nature of lesson study is that it provides a benchmarking process that teachers can use to gauge their own skills. Collaboration includes continuing interactions about effective teaching methods plus observations of one another's classrooms. These activities help teachers reflect on their own practice and identify things that can be improved. As researcher Catherine Lewis found, teacher collaboration can create a profound motivation to improve. A young teacher she interviewed recalled that after watching a lesson by her fellow first-grade teacher, she burst into tears: "I felt so sorry for my own students. I thought their lives would have been so much better if they'd been in the other teacher's class."[15]

At the same time, the collaborative nature of lesson study

balances the self-critiquing of individual teachers with the idea that improved teaching is a joint process, not the province or responsibility of any individual. This idea is embodied in the fact that when Japanese teachers plan a lesson collaboratively, they treat the result as a joint product whose ownership is shared by all in the group. When one teacher teaches the lesson and the others observe, problems that emerge are generally attributed to the lesson as designed by the group, not to the teacher who implemented the lesson. It thus becomes possible for teachers to be critical without offending their colleague. The discussion can focus more pointedly and deeply on the merits and deficiencies of the lesson, and on the process of revising and improving it. This leads us to our final point.

Teachers Who Participate in Lesson Study See Themselves as Contributing to the Development of Knowledge About Teaching as Well as to Their Own Professional Development

Teachers in Japan see themselves as developing the profession as well as themselves. Few U.S. teachers would feel this way. When U.S. teachers go to workshops and training seminars, they go to learn about a new activity or technique; most wouldn't conceive it possible that they might be making a contribution to the knowledge base of the teaching profession. The reason they feel this way is that, given our current system, they are right—they are not making such a contribution. In the U.S. system, it is researchers who are supposed to discover and recommend new teaching practices. Teachers are supposed to implement these practices in their classrooms, but alas, they usually fail to do so, much to the chagrin and disappointment of the educational research community. This predictably sets the stage for talk of how the teaching profession attracts a less-than-able subset of the U.S. workforce, and how, apparently, U.S. teachers are just not smart enough to do what researchers tell them to do.

But there is another possibility: Perhaps what teachers are told by researchers to do makes little sense in the context of an actual classroom. Researchers might be very smart. But they do not have access to the same information that teachers have as they confront real students in the context of real lessons with real learning goals. For researchers to improve teaching, they must guess at many of the things that are readily perceivable by teachers. And they probably guess wrong a good deal of the time.

Japan has succeeded in developing a system that not only develops teachers but also develops knowledge about teaching that is relevant to classrooms and sharable among the members of the teaching profession. Not only do lesson-study groups operate in individual schools, but the process of designing and critiquing research lessons is an integral part of the larger professional activity of both teachers and researchers. Professional conferences include sessions in which participants observe research lessons in local schools and then return to the conference meeting center for panel discussions of the lessons.[16] Although some education conferences in the United States include field trips to special demonstration schools for a small number of interested participants, the kind of broad-based intensive examination of individual lessons common in Japan is almost unknown in this country.

Through the process of improving lessons and sharing with colleagues the knowledge they acquire, something remarkable happens to teachers: They begin viewing themselves as true professionals. They see themselves as contributing to the knowledge base that defines the profession. And they see this as an integral part of what it means to be a teacher. As one Japanese teacher said, when asked why she invests so much effort in trying to improve lessons, "Why do we do research lessons? I don't think there are any laws. But if we didn't do research lessons, we wouldn't be teachers."[17]

Conclusions

Through the gradual improvement of individual lessons, and through the knowledge developed and shared during this process, the Japanese system enables the steady improvement of teachers and teaching. In Japan, educators can look back over the past fifty years and believe that teaching has improved. In the United States, we cannot do this. We can see fashions and trends, ups and downs. But we cannot see the kind of gradual improvement that marks true professions.

It is clear that we need a research-and-development system for the steady, continuous improvement of teaching; such a system does not exist today. We must move beyond models of reform in which we try to replace one teaching method with another by distributing the written recommendations of experts. Like the Yemeni immigrants in Shanker's story, we get teachers to use our tables, but they often turn those tables upside down. Instead, we must take the first step toward building a system that will, over time, lead to improvement of teaching and learning in the American classroom. We need new ideas for teaching, ideas such as those provided by the videos from Japan and Germany. But instead of copying these ideas we must feed them into our own research-and-development system for the improvement of classroom teaching. And we must empower teachers to be the leaders in this process. In the next chapter we lay out a concrete proposal for building such a system.

CHAPTER 8

Setting the Stage for Continuous Improvement

A
LTHOUGH THE HIGH achievement of Japanese students
has been a favorite media topic, Japan's system for
improving teaching has attracted little interest in the
United States. Perhaps this is because it is a program with little fanfare. Americans like to think big. Something as simple
and straightforward as lesson study just isn't dramatic enough
to capture the imagination of educational reformers in the
United States. "Wouldn't it take forever," a colleague asks, "to
improve teaching one lesson at a time?" "Our kids need help
now, not ten years from now," says a politician. "We need
major restructuring, not modest improvements." Yet despite
our desperate rush to reform, the evidence shows that little has
changed inside U.S. classrooms. By trying to accomplish too
much, we have sacrificed opportunities for small, cumulative
improvements.

Japan, in contrast, has attached great value to small improvements. Like the tortoise, Japan has pinned its hopes on steady
progress, not on momentous leaps forward. There is nothing
magical about the modest changes Japanese teachers devise in

their lesson-study groups. Indeed, U.S. teachers would surely come up with equally good ideas, given the opportunity. What is most impressive about Japan is that the culture genuinely values what teachers know, learn, and invent, and has developed a system to take advantage of teachers' ideas: evaluating them, adapting them, accumulating them into a professional knowledge base, and sharing them. The Japanese have created a national research-and-development system, based on teachers' experiences, that ensures the gradual improvement of teaching over time.

Is it possible to build such a system here in the United States? Our answer is yes, and the time to build such a system is now. A system of gradual improvement like that found in Japan depends on clear standards for what students should learn and means of assessing progress toward meeting the standards. These have been lacking in the United States up to now, but this is changing rapidly. Most states have set new, high standards for what students must learn. The problem now is to find ways to meet these standards.

We believe that the key to meeting the new standards is to improve teaching. The same curricula and teaching methods we have been using will no longer suffice. In this chapter and the next we propose a system of gradual improvement in teaching over time. We believe that if teaching can be improved—not just in special locations but inside the average classroom—student learning will follow. Even though we have seen that teaching, as a cultural system, can be difficult to change, the case of Japan shows that change is possible.

The core of our proposal is to establish something like Japan's lesson-study system here in the United States. Many readers will no doubt be skeptical that a program developed in another culture can be instituted here. Certainly, we do not expect the system that evolves here to be identical to the one that has evolved in Japan. Our system differs from the Japanese system in critical ways; not least among them is the lack of a national curriculum. Because no system of gradual improvement has ever been tried in this country on a national scale before, much will have to be tested and refined over time. Our goal is simply to convince the reader that something like lesson study deserves to be tested seriously in the United States. It is our hypothesis that if our educational system can find a way to use lesson study for building professional knowledge of teaching, teaching and learning will improve.

Improvement will not happen by itself. It will require designing and building a research-and-development system that explicitly targets steady, gradual improvement of teaching and learning. Like the Japanese, we must be able to look back ten or twenty years from now and clearly see that we have improved—gradually but continuously. We cannot make such a statement today. What kind of system will allow us do so in the future?

Six Principles for Gradual, Measurable Improvement

We propose six principles that must be taken seriously by anyone attempting to improve teaching. It is not coincidental that these principles are largely congruent with the key features of lesson study enumerated in Chapter 7. We note here, and again later, that lesson study is one process that is fully consistent with these principles. Indeed, that is why we are optimistic about the benefits that will accrue if lesson study can become part of the U.S. educational system.

Principle #1: Expect Improvement to Be Continual, Gradual, and Incremental

Because teaching is a system that is deeply embedded in the surrounding culture of schools, any changes will come in small steps, not in dramatic leaps.[1] History supports this claim: In spite of waves of reform that have called for sudden, major shifts, teaching has always evolved like other complex, culturally embedded activities—slowly and incrementally.[2] Dramatic and fundamental changes can occur, even at the core, but these will result from accumulating small changes over time.

This means that we must take a long-term view when we design initiatives for improving teaching. We must reset our expectations, cultivated over a century of school reform, and anticipate slow and steady improvement, not momentous change. Efforts to reform teaching overnight, or even over a few years, are unlikely to have their intended effect. In addition, we must learn to value small improvements. Small improvements often are derided as "too little, too late" and are killed off before they have a chance to build into something significant. Teachers must be allowed and encouraged to invent small changes in the system of teaching and then to keep track of these changes so they can be accumulated and shared.

Principle #2: Maintain a Constant Focus on Student Learning Goals

The goal of teaching is students' learning. The goal of improving teaching is improving students' learning. Too often, however, reformers forget the goals of reform, gauging their success by changes in the particular forms of teaching. Bruce Joyce and colleagues, who have been involved in school reform for some time, have noted: "The centrality of student learning becomes lost as the details of program implementation become ends in themselves."[3] The question of whether and how these changes are improving students' learning in the teacher's classroom gets lost in the sheer effort to change.

Improving complex systems, such as teaching, requires a relentless focus on the bottom-line goals—in this case, students' learning—and a commitment to evaluate changes with respect to these goals. Such a focus appears to be a necessary component of any successful school improvement program. Listen again to Bruce Joyce and his colleagues: "In all reported cases of school improvement initiatives in which substantial student learning occurred, school staff kept students' interests as learners central throughout the planning, implementation, and assessment phases. We did not find a single case in the literature where student learning increased but had not been a central goal."[4]

Principle #3: Focus on Teaching, Not Teachers

A number of recent efforts to improve classroom instruction have targeted the competency of teachers.[5] The National Board for Professional Teaching Standards, for example, has instituted a voluntary certification process to help raise the standards by which teachers are certified. Many states have instituted alternative certification programs designed to recruit high-achieving individuals without formal teacher training into the profession. Although we applaud the desire to raise standards for certification and to increase the pool of talented teachers, we believe that long-term improvement in teaching will depend more on the development of effective *methods for teaching* than on the identification and recruitment of talented individuals into the profession.

In biological evolution we know that it is the gene that is subject to natural selection, not the individual organism. Individuals are short-lived by evolutionary standards; they don't last long enough to undergo the slow process of evolutionary change. Genes, in contrast, persist over hundreds and thousands of generations. Teaching, similarly, persists, while teachers come and go. If we are to achieve long-term improvements in classroom teaching and learning, we must shift our focus from teachers to teaching. As we noted earlier, teachers follow scripts that they acquire as members of their culture, and their effectiveness depends on the scripts they use. Recruiting highly qualified teachers will not result in steady improvement as long as they continue to use the same scripts. It is the scripts that must be improved.

Principle #4: Make Improvements in Context

Goals give us the yardstick against which improvement can be measured. But how can we identify and develop ways to improve teaching? Because teaching is complex, improvements in teaching will be most successful if they are developed in the classrooms where teachers teach and students learn. Teaching is a system built from all the elements of the local context: teacher, students, curriculum, and so on. Improving the system requires taking all of these elements into account. What works in one classroom might or might not work in another classroom. Ideas for improvement that come from afar—including, for example, what we've learned from Japanese lessons—will need to be tested and adapted to our own local classrooms if they are to have any chance of success. Teaching is unlikely to improve through researchers' developing innovations in one place and then prescribing them for everyone. Innovations can spread around the country, but only by trying them out and adjusting them again and again as they encounter different kinds of classrooms.

Educators have become increasingly aware of the importance of context in understanding and facilitating learning, but the arguments have been applied more often to students' learning than to teachers' learning.[6] Teaching, given its systemic, cultural nature, is especially sensitive to context—a good reason to take advantage of the very contexts in which teachers function every day. Teachers learning in the classrooms and schools in which they teach is an idea that has been proposed for some time, yet most teachers have not realized this opportunity.[7] It certainly contrasts with many traditional methods of teacher development (for example, weekend workshops, university courses) in which teachers are expected to learn something new, disconnected from their context, then hope it works when they take it back to their classrooms.

Principle #5: Make Improvement the Work of Teachers

One way to ensure that improvements can be developed in context is to entrust change to those engaged in the activity—classroom teachers. Improving something as complex and culturally embedded as teaching requires the efforts of all the players, including students, parents, and politicians. But teachers must be the primary driving force behind change. They are best positioned to understand the problems that students face and to generate possible solutions. In fact, almost all successful attempts to improve teaching have involved teachers working together to improve students' learning.[8]

A second reason for making improvement the work of teachers is that there are so many teachers, especially when compared with the number of educational researchers. If we can find a way to marshal the efforts and experiences of our 2.5 million classroom teachers, the potential is far greater than anything that could be achieved by a few thousand researchers.

Teachers should be engaged in improvement because they are the only ones who can ensure that students' learning improves. They are the gatekeepers of the classrooms in which teaching and learning take place. As we pointed out earlier, the classroom is the final common channel through which all efforts to improve school learning must flow. We cannot *not* work with teachers. They are, necessarily, the solution to the problem of improving teaching.

Principle #6: Build a System That Can Learn from Its Own Experience

Each day, vast numbers of U.S. teachers solve problems, try new approaches, and develop their own knowledge of what works and what doesn't work in their own classrooms. Yet we have no way to harvest what even the most brilliant teachers have learned, no way to share that knowledge and use it to advance the professional knowledge base of teaching. U.S. teachers work alone, for the most part, and when they retire, all that they have learned is lost to the profession. Each new generation of teachers must start from scratch, finding its own way.

If efforts to improve schools are going to add up to more than just a temporary fix, it is necessary to find a way to accumulate knowledge about teaching and to share this knowledge with new practitioners entering the teaching profession. In the long run, of course, we need to change the teaching scripts that govern classroom practice. Scripts themselves might be the most effective means of storing professional knowledge. But scripts will not be changed unless we have a knowledge base to support the change. We must build a system with a memory, in other words, one that provides a means of accumulating the experiences and insights of teachers. Without this, there is no way of getting better over time.

Initiatives for Change: Setting the Stage

The six principles proposed above are consistent with what we have learned about teaching. But principles alone will not bring about change. We must formulate action plans, based on these principles, to guide the work of school improvement over time. Because the United States has no tradition of gradual improvement, we must test the plans, monitor their level of success, and use the information to refine them over time. To begin the process, we propose a program based squarely on the process of lesson study, a program that we believe, if implemented, will produce long-term steady improvements in students' learning.

Establishing the program we envision is a monumental task, not so much because it is costly or requires new resources but because it involves a change in school culture. Changes in cultures, as we have noted many times, do not happen overnight. It is not that schools in the United States cannot improve classroom practice. Indeed, the program we propose shares many features with a number of local school improvement efforts that have shown great success.[9] The problem is that these successes have never reached far beyond the sites receiving special attention and assistance. They certainly have not touched the average school and the average teacher.[10]

Simply recommending lesson study as a useful process is not enough, because the process cannot succeed, on a wide scale, without a supporting context. In the remainder of this chapter, we propose three initiatives in the form of school district tasks that must accompany the introduction of lesson study. The initiatives are directed toward creating cultures in schools and districts that would support any long-term teacher-driven improvement process, including lesson study. For each initiative, we describe the roles that must be played by the primary stakeholders—school boards, superintendents, principals, teachers, and parents.

Remember, our current system for improving teaching, just like the system of classroom teaching, is a cultural activity. As such, it will change gradually, just as teaching itself does. To succeed, we must be able to start small but also be able to expand. Whatever research-and-development system we construct to improve teaching over time must be capable of working even for a single district, for that is where such change will inevitably start. But there also must be a clear means of growing the system into one that can serve the nation as a whole.

Initiative #1: Build Consensus for Continuous Improvement

Who, in a school district, is in the best position to start the process of improving teaching? There is no single answer, because each district is different. Teachers, of course, are essential for the success of any effort. But it is rare for teachers to have the opportunity and time to lead such an effort. There must be involvement from the very top, especially from the school board. Principals will have difficulty starting such a process by themselves unless they have the unqualified support of their superintendents. Superintendents are a logical choice to lead the change, and they definitely will play a major role. But typically, they don't last long enough in their positions to follow through over long periods of time.[11] School boards, though historically ineffective in leading reform efforts, have the power to make a real difference if they so choose.[12] To be effective, school boards must build political consensus and public support for long-term improvement and then commit resources for many years to the task of improving students' learning.

Building consensus around a process of slow, gradual improvement will not be easy. Traditionally, Americans have been more willing to accept dramatic failures than to applaud, or even appreciate, small successes. It seems as if we have an all-or-nothing culture: We want results fast or we are not interested. Gradual change, although it is the working model in Japan, has not been an option for many Americans.

In order to sell a model of gradual improvement to all stakeholders, outcome measures must be developed that are sophisticated enough to detect small changes in student learning and to differentiate such changes from random fluctuations. As students' learning gradually improves, it will be easier for school boards to strengthen the district's resolve to work hard for small improvements. It is important for school board members to remember that alternative paths, driven by impatience, have not worked well. The evidence suggests that efforts to produce rapid, wholesale change have failed to improve schools in virtually every case.[13] It's time to start a realistic program of improvement.

Initiative #2: Set Clear Learning Goals for Students and Align Assessments with These Goals

We hear a lot these days about standards. Much of the discussion, at least when politicians are involved, refers to how high or low standards are, and to the importance of raising them. But standards involve a great deal more than simply high expectations. Standards contain the goals that we value most. And clear goals for what we want students to learn are essential. Without them, it is not possible to set a course toward improvement. Without clear goals, we also cannot know whether changes represent improvement or . . . just change.

Not only must there be clear goals, but if teachers are going to collaborate to find ways of improving instruction, the goals must be widely accepted. Most high-achieving countries have national goals for student learning. Japan, for example, has an explicit set of mathematics-learning goals for all of its students, grade by grade. When a Japanese teacher group works on improving lessons, it is not working alone. Many teacher groups throughout Japan are working on lessons with the same goals in mind. This means they can easily share the products of their efforts.

In the United States, we do not have national learning goals, and in some cases, we do not even share a set of learning goals within a district. We tend to rationalize this situation by referring to local and individual needs of different groups of students in different parts of the country and even in different schools and classrooms. Although local contexts might differ in some respects, we must realize that a set of shared learning and curricular goals is a minimum requirement for teachers to collaborate effectively. This does not mean that we must enforce, or even adopt, a set of national goals, but it does mean that we must, at least, develop shared goals at the district level.

Fortunately, there is a growing consensus around the country regarding the importance of developing clear learning and curricular goals for all students. As we noted in Chapter 1, the standards set by various professional organizations and the standards being developed within individual states have moved this activity to the top of the educational agenda. The National Science Board, an independent national science advisory panel established by the U.S. Congress in 1950, recently issued a statement urging "all stakeholders in our vast grass-roots system of K–12 education to develop a nation-wide consensus for a common core of knowledge and competency in mathematics and science."[14] In the short run, it will be difficult to develop a national consensus on learning goals, but a district-wide consensus surely can be achieved.

Some thought must be given to the way in which learning goals are stated. Goals can emphasize skills (for example, "students should be able to add two three-digit numbers"), or they can emphasize conceptual understanding ("students should understand how the place value nature of numbers allows different methods of adding to work equally well"). They can be short-term or long-term. They also can be at various levels of generality. For example, they might refer to "being able to perform basic arithmetic operations on whole numbers" or "being able to add single-digit numbers whose sum is less than ten." There is no one correct way to define learning goals. What is important, first, is that goals capture the kind of learning that we most value and, second, that they are clear enough to link directly to the lessons, units, and grade levels that make up a curriculum.

Who should develop shared goals for student learning? Because such goals should be district-wide at least, superintendents must take a leadership role. But the development of *shared* goals will require participation of parents, principals, and especially teachers. Districts can take advantage of the best work that has already been done at the state and national levels in setting clear goals pitched at an appropriate level of specificity.

The process of attaching meaning to the learning goals is a long one requiring a great deal of work by teachers. A learning goal is not easily defined and not easily summarized in a written document. The true meaning of learning goals becomes apparent only as teachers link them to assessments and weave them into a coherent curriculum and use them to guide their teaching decisions.

Assessments must be aligned with goals. Often, assessments are linked to goals for purposes of accountability, but assessments play an essential role in the improvement process. Even with clear goals, teachers cannot improve their practice unless they have access to a steady flow of information about the effectiveness of their teaching. As teachers engage in continual assessment of their students' learning, they will gradually develop understandings of how students learn from classroom instruction, and they will begin to perceive direct links between the goals they set, their own teaching, and their students' learning. With this information, teachers are in a good position to work together to improve their lessons.

Initiative #3: Restructure Schools as Places Where Teachers Can Learn

A little-recognized truth in educational reform is that every recommendation for improving teaching requires teachers to learn.[15] This is not surprising. Changing one's practice in any professional field requires examining the old and new practices, making the appropriate modifications, and learning to carry out new practices effectively. It would be silly to expect teachers to simply execute improved teaching methods without providing them with opportunities to develop these methods and learn how to use them.

If we expect teachers to play a major role in improving

instruction, as they must, then we need to provide an environment in which they can do this work. Unfortunately, the vast majority of American schools are not suited to this purpose. Teachers work alone, for the most part, and have little time to interact, much less collaborate. They arrive at school shortly before the students do and leave shortly after the students leave. While at school, teachers spend most of their time teaching.

This may sound perfectly fine to many people. Aren't teachers paid to teach? Aren't teachers already trained in college and certified to teach? Why should they be doing anything else in school? Yet other professions that involve complex skills, such as law or medicine, expect their members to become more skilled over time and provide opportunities for learning new skills. This is true even for professions that often are assumed to require less training. Albert Shanker noted that the new process for building cars introduced by Saturn provides ninety-two hours of reeducation per year for each employee. Shanker said, "It is ironic that a bunch of people whose business is building cars understand so well the importance of educating their employees, whereas people in education seem to assume that teachers and other school staff will be able to step right into a new way of doing things with little or no help. If it takes . . . 92 hours a year per employee to make a better automobile, it will take that and more to make better schools."[16]

But the common American view of teaching does not include learning to teach while teaching. We typically expect that most teachers will be doing pretty much the same things in their classrooms when they are veteran teachers as when they begin teaching; in fact, some people believe that beginning teachers might be more effective, entering the profession with fresh ideas. And given the lack of learning opportunities for teachers, they might be right.

Improving teaching is not something that can be left to refresher courses in the evenings or during the summer in university classrooms. Improving teaching must be done at school, in classrooms, and it must be seen by teachers, parents, and administrators as a substantial and important part of the teacher's workweek. Schools must be places where teachers, as well as students, can learn.

Changing schools to support teachers' learning requires changing the culture of schools. We have emphasized culture as an important idea for understanding why teaching looks the way it does and why it is resistant to change. The reader could get the impression that it is impossible to change teaching because there are so many cultural factors that keep it in place. It is crucial, at this point, to distinguish between the wider American culture and the culture of schools. They are related, but they are not the same. What is needed to improve teaching is a change in *school* culture, and this *is* possible. Witness the individual schools and districts around the country that *are* changing.[17]

A requirement for beginning the change process is finding time during the workweek for teachers to collaborate. In our opinion, two hours per week is a reasonable goal, at least initially. Time is a precious commodity in teachers' schedules, and finding time for teachers to work together presents a challenge to the typical school district.[18] Many people assume that the cost associated with doing so would be prohibitive. But there are low-cost solutions that can work and that are working in a number of school districts across the country. Some of these solutions are based on the fact that nonteaching personnel now account for more than half of the U.S. education workforce, a percentage that has increased steadily since World War II and that far exceeds the proportion of nonteaching personnel in most other countries.[19] If funding can be shifted into teaching, and away from nonteaching personnel, it is possible to free teachers to devote significant amounts of time each week to the improvement of teaching.

In a recent book, Linda Darling-Hammond presents one analysis of how this can be accomplished.[20] Darling-Hammond analyzed the way staff time is allocated in typical high schools and found that only 33 percent of the time was dedicated to teaching. By eliminating bureaucratic staff and adding teachers, some schools have been able to reduce class size and create up to ten hours per week for each teacher to invest in individual and collaborative efforts to improve teaching. And all of this has been accomplished without an increase in the overall cost of education. Darling-Hammond cites as an example the case of New York City's Community District 2. In this district, professional development has been targeted as the highest priority, and the school has been restructured to provide time for teacher collaboration and even cross-school observations by teachers. Student achievement has gone up.

Some districts have been able to implement such changes in personnel quite quickly. For others this might be a long-term solution, as staff retirees are replaced by teachers and as teachers' jobs are redefined. For these latter districts, a more appealing short-term solution might be to review the current workday schedule along with all the in-service opportunities for teachers and to restructure these into regular collaborative work time.[21] Principals and superintendents will need to take the lead in reorganizing schedules and in-service activities.

This much can be achieved without additional resources. The changes require only redirecting funds already spent operating our schools. Now imagine what would happen if we were to take the millions of dollars spent every year to *reform* American education, much of which has little affect on classroom practice, and use it to provide the time and resources teachers need to improve teaching. We would have plenty of funds to support a vigorous, highly focused research-and-development system. The evidence suggests that this would be a wise change in how we spend reform money: increased spending on teacher education has a greater positive effect on student learning than increased spending on other school variables.[22]

It is becoming clear that the district is the unit that can restructure most successfully. As was noted earlier, the district is small enough that it should be possible to achieve consensus on students' learning goals and to implement a common curriculum. At the same time, the district level is large enough to allow substantive restructuring in terms of funding and staff allocations. The district office is usually the site of budgetary control. The district also is the level at which superintendents and school boards can exert strong leadership.

A final reason that restructuring should be done at the district level is that a district-wide program provides teachers with a critical but often overlooked opportunity for professional growth. Teachers must have the opportunity to enlarge their horizons beyond their own classrooms and their own schools. We are asking them to undertake a significant task: to improve the quality of teaching as part of a nationwide effort. To do more than improve teaching in their own classrooms, to raise the standard of good teaching within the profession— this demands that teachers work together, sharing what they learn in their classrooms to help one another learn even more. It demands that they assume responsibility for building the profession's knowledge base. Working with teachers from their own and other schools will allow them to develop this critical new professional perspective.

Summary

If these first three initiatives can be implemented, the stage will be ready for long-term, steady improvement. These are not initiatives that can be launched by a single teacher inside a single classroom, but they *can* be set in motion by a single school district. They will be sustained only with strong leadership at the highest levels of the community and broad participation by the school board, superintendent, principals, teachers, and parents.

Even implementing these critical three initiatives, however, will not, in and of itself, produce gains in student achievement. For this we must make substantive changes inside classrooms, at the place where student learning occurs. Once teachers have time during their workweek to devote to the improvement of teaching, what should they do with this time? We turn to this question in the next chapter.

CHAPTER 9

The Steady Work of Improving Teaching

O NCE A DISTRICT has laid out an organizational structure for school improvement, with time for teachers to work in collaborative groups, what should teachers do with their newfound time? Many reformers who thought increased planning time, by itself, would lead to improvements in teaching have found that it does not.[1] Indeed, teachers who are told simply to collaborate often find that they are not sure what they are supposed to do, or how such collaborations can help them to improve their teaching. One school district that restructured to allow teachers time to collaborate found within months that teachers were complaining about the time they were supposed to spend meeting together. "Let's just go home early," said one of the teachers, "and use the time at home to prepare for tomorrow's lessons."

This is not teachers' fault; it merely demonstrates the fact that although most people now agree that teachers need opportunities for professional development, there is a dearth of knowledge about the process by which teachers actually learn to improve their practice. We are attracted to the Japanese notion of lesson study because it lays out a clear model for teacher learning and a clear set of principles or hypotheses about how teachers learn. Lesson study embodies a set of concrete steps that teachers can take, over time, to improve teaching. These steps may need to be modified to work in the United States. But we believe it is better to start with an explicit model, even if it needs revising, than with no model at all.

Which is why, in this chapter, we propose lesson study, American-style, as the foundation of our efforts to improve teaching in this country. We describe our vision of how lesson study can work for U.S. teachers. Lesson study, as it works in Japan, is fully consistent with what we know about how to improve complex cultural activities like teaching, and it works, simultaneously, toward improving both teaching and teachers' knowledge and skills. This means it could lead to the kind of continuing improvement in learning that American students deserve. The process is not magical or sudden, and it will encounter some significant challenges. It will be, above all, steady work.[2] Our task is to explore through planning, implementation, and reflection how lesson study can grow and adapt to become a functioning research-and-development system for the improvement of teaching in the United States.

Can Lesson Study Work in the United States?

Before we rush to implement a lesson-study program for the United States, we pause to question whether such a plan could work in the United States at all. There are several reasons to suppose that it could. For one, the features of lesson study, as practiced in Japan, are very similar to those reported by American researchers as characterizing successful experimental teacher-development programs.[3] Reports of American school-based improvement initiatives that include such features—for example, setting goals for students' learning, working together to improve practice, attending to the curriculum and students' thinking—indicate that teaching can be improved by programs that resemble lesson study. Lesson study also is consistent with another, gradually expanding, movement that is often referred to by the phrase "teacher-as-researcher."[4] One of the goals of this movement is to encourage teachers to engage in research, thereby creating in the teacher a temperament oriented to inquiry and a disposition toward investigating one's own practice. Such a disposition is at the heart of the lesson-study process.

But such evidence is weak, at best. What works on a small scale in experimental settings almost never scales up, especially in education. Many teachers in the United States do not even prepare lesson plans, at least not around student learning goals.[5] Why would they suddenly be willing to engage in lesson study? For lesson study to be a viable means of improving teaching nationwide, it must be able to flourish and grow within the current educational landscape. For this to happen, two tests must be passed. First, lesson study must meet the needs of teachers. Teachers must be motivated to engage in lesson study. They must be willing to try it, and once it is started, they must find it relevant and useful to the problems they face each day in the classroom. Only then will they continue to participate. Second, lesson study must fit within the current political and policy contexts that surround American education; in other words, it must meet the needs of the U.S. education system. Teachers are under great pressure to perform, and the stakes keep getting higher. Lesson study must meet the needs that teachers have to meet these pressures.

Meeting Teachers' Needs

Teaching is a difficult and demanding job. Teachers are isolated from their colleagues and rarely have the opportunity to participate in professional life outside the classroom. They are pressed by administrators and reformers to take on new responsibilities, to teach in new ways, and to show better results. But they are given few resources to meet these demands. Lesson study is not just another activity that teachers must add to the list of expectations, it is a way for teachers to deal with these expectations. Lesson study is a comprehensive program that can provide teachers with opportunities for practice-based professional development that, until now, they have been denied.

With its detailed analysis of practice and its frequent observations of other teachers, lesson study provides benchmarks against which teachers can measure their own practice and compare it with that of their colleagues. These comparisons, more than any external rewards, can create in teachers a strong desire to improve their own practice. As teachers watch other teachers, it is possible for them to imagine new possibilities for their own teaching. Lesson study provides a concrete means of trying out these possibilities in a nonthreatening context with the help of colleagues. This personal motivation is, in the end, the kind of demand that will produce improved teaching.

Some may question whether, even if they become motivated to participate in lesson study, teachers have the capabilities to handle its demands. In our view, lesson study is not the kind of process in which teachers must first develop a list of capabilities and then begin to design improved lessons. Lesson study is, in fact, the ideal context in which teachers *develop* deeper and broader capabilities. This is what we mean when we say that lesson study is a form of teacher development as well as a program for improving teaching.

Suppose, for example, that a group of fifth-grade teachers wants to improve an introductory lesson on decimal fractions. As part of the process, teachers would engage in research. They might consult other texts, invite special consultants for this aspect of their work, or meet with other teachers in the school or district. They might also study how students think about decimal fractions, and try to use this knowledge to predict how students would respond to various instructional alternatives. Through all of these activities, teachers would be increasing their own knowledge of decimal fractions, and doing so in a way directly relevant to the improvement of their ability to teach the subject. In many ways, teachers' learning more about mathematics in the context of lesson study is preferable to taking another mathematics course at a neighboring college, because the teachers have a concrete and compelling reason for learning more about *this* topic. Much of what they learn can be connected to other aspects of teaching the topic—the tasks selected for students, the kinds of discussions that will be beneficial, and so on.

Lesson Study in the U.S. Context

If we assume that lesson study can meet teachers' needs, we still must examine how it fits within the U.S. education context. To succeed, lesson study must connect both to the curriculum of the school and to the current policy context in which teachers work.

Curriculum. In Japan, where there is a national curriculum, it makes sense to spend sustained periods of time perfecting a small set of lessons. Because all teachers teach the same curriculum, knowledge generated by one lesson-study group is usable by everyone who teaches at the same grade level. But the United States does not have a national curriculum.

Although the absence of a national curriculum will shape the nature of lesson study in the United States, it will not prevent lesson study from succeeding. The key is that the group of teachers who undertake lesson study must work from a shared curriculum. We have suggested that at the least, this must be done within the school district. As districts that use the same curriculum connect, teachers can share their results across district boundaries. In this sense, the same opportunity offered by Japan's national curriculum is available, though in a more limited fashion, to U.S. teachers.

Standards, Assessment, and Accountability. In today's policy context, curriculum is increasingly aligned with content standards and assessments. Teachers, more and more, are working within contexts in which they are accountable for students' performance on assessments. Lesson study is unique in its potential connection to local standards and assessment. Because improvements are curriculum-based, lesson study allows teachers to devote their time to improvements that align with their local standards and for which they are held accountable.

The traditional researchers' method for testing improvements—running an experiment that pits the new lessons against the old—is hardly possible in a teacher's ongoing instructional program. But if lesson study is a district-wide activity, teachers can compare their own results with those obtained by colleagues elsewhere in the district or in other districts. The most important results pertain to the quality of students' thinking and learning during the lesson. Provided appropriate assessment systems are in place, feedback from different classrooms can be used to discard the new lessons or to revise them and make them even better. Repeating the lessons with other students, in other contexts, is a quality-control process that works slowly, but it is a powerful process that assures teachers that improvements will occur gradually and continuously.

Connecting Policy with Classroom Practice. Finally, lesson study has the potential to solve what has been identified as a major problem in U.S. education, and that is the gap that exists between educational policymakers and classroom practice. Teachers are caught in a persistent dilemma: Although they frequently receive advice and recommendations on how to change their teaching, and they know that some of these changes would probably benefit their students, they also lack the learning opportunities needed to study the recommendations, decide which changes would be meaningful, and learn how to implement them. This leads teachers to devalue suggestions proposed by outsiders such as researchers or policymakers, because they fail to see them as relevant to their everyday classroom practice. And those who suggest the changes seldom get continuing feedback from teachers.

An example of the teacher's dilemma has been prompted by today's reform recommendations in mathematics and science. These recommendations ask teachers to teach in a more adventurous, ambitious way. Rather than demonstrating procedures for solving problems and then giving students worksheets of problems to practice, they are asked to present challenging problems to students and encourage students to develop their own methods of solution. Then they are to engage students in a thoughtful discussion of the alternative procedures, analyzing the pros and cons of each.[6] When well executed, this method of teaching has been shown to be quite effective.[7] But unless one knows what to expect from students, it is a scary way to teach. Success depends on making many split-second decisions about which student suggestions to follow up on and which to ignore.

What is learned by students during the lesson seems to depend on whether students hit upon the solution methods that make for good class discussions. Teachers can feel that they have lost control of the lesson, but they are told to "embrace the uncertainty," because this is what better teaching is like.[8]

Lesson study offers an alternative that will appeal to the teachers caught in this difficult position. Lesson study shifts the key for effective teaching from on-the-fly decision making during the lesson to careful investigation and planning before the lesson. Through the lesson-study process, teachers can collect information about how students are likely to respond to the challenging problems, and they can plan which responses to introduce into the discussion in which order. They can thereby orchestrate a rich discussion without the debilitating uncertainty with which they previously had to deal. Of course, some decisions still will need to be made extemporaneously, but good advance planning shoulders much of the burden. Indeed, planning takes on new value as a premier teaching skill. And participation in lesson study allows teachers to improve their planning skills over time.

Thus, what starts as a vague and impractical suggestion from educational experts gets transformed, through lesson study, into an improvement in classroom practice. By communicating the results of this improvement, teachers, researchers, and policymakers all increase their power to contribute to the improvement of education.

Establishing the Lesson-Study Process

The fact that lesson study could provide the key ingredient for improving students' learning, district by district, across the United

States does not mean it will be easy to implement. Even if the initiatives presented in the previous chapter are undertaken to provide a supportive context for continuous improvement, and even if the participants endorse the potential of lesson study, principals and teachers still face many challenges.

Leadership for Lesson Study

One of the biggest problems schools will face is that there are few leaders among its teachers for launching this process. Very few teachers have experienced this kind of professional development. Most teachers, as we have noted, work alone, in isolation from their colleagues. Those who do collaborate with other teachers generally do everything *except* work on the improvement of classroom lessons.

In the absence of experienced teacher leaders, principals must take an active role in introducing lesson study. The principal must become personally and directly involved in beginning the process and establishing it as a permanent part of the school program. The principal's involvement is one way to signal that improving teaching is the most critical part of the school's development. The principal must work closely with teachers and must nurture teacher leaders who are willing to devote considerable time and energy to the lesson-study process. Even when teachers step up to take more and more responsibility, the principal must remain active in maintaining the school's long-term commitment to the process. This means that the principal needs to understand and believe in the six principles that we proposed in the previous chapter. The principal must expect improvement to be gradual and continual, which will not be easy. The principal will need the support of other principals in the district as he or she rethinks current in-service practices and finds creative ways to institutionalize the structures and support necessary for this process to become a new way of doing business.

Of course, building a culture and tradition of lesson study in schools cannot depend solely on the principal. Teachers must begin to assume more and more leadership and responsibility. There are two leverage points in the U.S. educational system for encouraging this to happen. One is preservice education. Currently there are no teacher-preparation programs, of which we are aware, that engage students in a collaborative lesson-study experience. Thus, lesson study is a new concept for teachers entering the profession. If undergraduate methods courses were restructured to introduce students to collaboratively planning and testing lessons, new teachers would be ready to assume leadership roles more quickly. Collaboratively planning lessons means something very different from the traditional American exercise of writing lesson plans (an exercise with which most preservice teachers are too familiar). As was described in Chapter 7, lesson study includes setting clear learning goals, selecting and sequencing tasks by *anticipating* students' responses (and doing research, if necessary, to identify these responses), and planning the class discussions to build on students' responses and highlight the major points. These are challenging activities, but many undergraduate methods courses would benefit from taking them seriously.

As we noted earlier, preservice education, no matter how effective, cannot by itself produce continuous improvement. Continuous improvement requires ongoing opportunities to learn and improve while teaching. A second leverage point for jump-starting the lesson-study process is located in the field, where teaching occurs. As a program of school-based lesson study is getting started, it might help to bring in outside consultants to provide initial momentum and guidance. Even in Japan, where there is a fifty-year tradition of lesson study, many study groups work with an outside consultant. Such arrangements can provide additional focus and new ideas for the group. It must be remembered, however, that eventually teachers must lead the process and consultants must be just that—consultants. This means that there needs to be a strategic plan for preparing and supporting teachers to become leaders of lesson-study groups.

Districts might begin the process of lesson study by inviting two teachers from each school to work intensively with a consultant who has the knowledge and skills to develop school leaders for lesson study. These teacher leaders, over time, would start lesson-study groups within their own schools but maintain their relations with leaders in other schools. Each school is different, and we cannot predict where the leaders will come from in any school. But because improving students' learning must be the number-one concern of each school's principal, the principal must assign priority to developing leadership for the improvement of teaching.

Making It Work

Lesson study is, at its core, a teacher activity. Teachers must make it work. True, it is impossible for teachers to initiate and sustain a vigorous program of lesson study without the active support of the school board, superintendent, principal, and parents. But the success of the activity ultimately depends on teachers.

The actual process of lesson study might take a variety of forms, depending on the mission and goal of the school, the learning goals set for students, the teachers' interests, and so on. However, some general guidelines can be suggested to keep the activity focused on the primary goal of improving classroom lessons to increase students' learning.

We already have identified time as an essential requirement. For teacher groups to make measurable progress in their efforts to improve lessons, they need two hours per week of uninterrupted study. This must be a priority in school scheduling.

Groups can be formed on the basis of shared interests, shared problems, common curriculum expectations, or other criteria that make sense for planning common lessons. The school's sixth-grade mathematics teachers might form a group to design several lessons on introducing ratio and proportion. Or interested teachers of grades seven and eight might form a group to plan a sequence of lessons on the democratic election process. All the groups should have explicit goals that are consistent with the mission of the school. Groups of three to five members are ideal. Schools might announce the study groups for the year, perhaps following a planning phase. Teachers might sign up for a group of their choice or might be asked to serve on a group by the principal or a teacher committee.

Deciding on the goals for lesson-study groups is an important first step. Many factors might come into play during this planning stage, but one important factor always should be teachers' judgments of the problems that impede students' learning. The goal of lesson study is to improve students' learning, so it makes sense to begin by addressing those topics and issues that are most in need of improvement. The problems students face might be formidable, but they are not random. For example, most fourth-grade teachers would report problems in their students' understanding of fractions. When teachers within a district are working with a shared curriculum, they will find commonality in the problems they face for given topics and given grade levels. Identifying such problems is an ideal way to start the lesson-study process.

Once they have identified a common problem, the group needs to select a particular lesson in which that problem can be addressed. Usually this will be a lesson they have taught before but with which they are not satisfied. The group must then spend time in the beginning clarifying in detail what the learning goal for the lesson is and how they will know that they have achieved it. They also should try to understand how the goal of the lesson fits into district and state standards and assessment systems. Neither the problem nor the learning goal needs to be overly ambitious. The aim is to produce small but solid improvements in one or two lessons with modest goals. Japanese teachers, who have engaged in this process for many years, often redesign only two or three lessons over the year.

Once a lesson has been identified, the group can develop an overall work plan for the year. The plan for the year should allocate initial time for finding out more about how students learn the concepts in question, determining what others recommend for teaching these concepts effectively, and learning more about the concepts themselves. The balance of the plan should then include time for designing improved lessons, trying them out with students, collecting information regarding their success, revising the lessons accordingly, and repeating the cycle. The plan should also include time for the group to write a report of their work to be shared with colleagues.

Notice that part of the annual activity is researching and discussing others' recommendations for effective teaching of particular topics. This activity can resolve a long-standing problem for American educational reform. As we noted earlier, simply distributing written documents compiled by researchers and curriculum developers has been notoriously unsuccessful for improving practice. It is not that the written documents are deficient; they might contain excellent ideas. The problem is that the American system makes no provision for teachers to digest these recommendations and translate them into practice. In our opinion, lesson study is an ideal process for gradually working through new recommendations and giving them life in the classroom.

Building an Infrastructure for Sharing Professional Knowledge

If we implement lesson study, we will have started the process of continuous improvement. The next challenge is to move from improving teaching practice in individual classrooms and individual schools to improving teaching across the country. The key questions are: "How do teachers, collectively, improve the common standard of teaching? How do they build a professional knowledge base for teaching?" The answers lie in finding ways for teachers to share what they are learning in their individual study groups. Large-scale improvements, over time, in the quality of classroom instruction can result only if teachers can effectively communicate their discoveries to their colleagues, both present and future.

Finding effective ways to share knowledge about teaching is not a simple task. Previous approaches to this problem, such as codifying principles about teaching in reports and policy documents, have led to disappointing results. As we found in the TIMSS video study, teachers rarely interpret such documents in the ways intended by the authors, and have difficulty adapting the ideas into the realities of classroom life. On the other hand, approaches that stress the sharing of specific tips and techniques often lead to superficial changes that are disconnected from students' learning. In the next section we argue that one of the lasting benefits of lesson study is that the knowledge that results from lesson study is uniquely sharable.

Theories Linked with Examples

As was noted in the previous chapter, Japanese lesson-study groups have several ways of communicating the results of their work. The participating teachers teach some of their lessons publicly, inviting other teachers to watch. They also write case reports that describe the sequence of plans, outcomes, and revisions that their group has gone through. These case reports are then accumulated into larger books or stored in archives for easy access by other teachers.

The knowledge contained in these reports is quite different from what one finds in U.S. books about teaching. It is not made up of principles devoid of specific examples or examples without principles. It is *theories linked with examples*. This kind of knowledge is notable in several respects. First, theoretical insights are always linked with specific referents in the classroom. When a lesson-study group reports, for example, that one of its hypotheses has been supported, it is never outside the context of a specific lesson with specific goals, materials, students, and so on, all of which would be described in the report. At the same time, specific suggestions of how to teach are always justified by the teachers' theoretical analysis of what they have been investigating in their lesson-study group. This blend of theory and example gives other teachers the information they need to relate the group's work to their own classrooms and to think through what might be different in a different context.

The Japanese lesson-study groups' case reports also contain information about students' responses to the lessons the group has taught. We mention this not only because such information turns out to be quite powerful in the context of teacher planning activities but also because it highlights an interesting kind of research that has been well exploited by Japanese educators. It is worth noting that much of American educational psychology has focused on predicting individual responses to various materials and situations but has not had a great deal of success. The Japanese have taken a different approach: Although it is not easy to predict what any particular student will do in a given situation, it is quite easy to predict what a group of forty students will do. This is simply the result of the statistical principle of aggregation. Japanese teachers have ready access to information of the form "When presented with problem A, 60 percent of students will use Strategy One, 20 percent Strategy Two, 15 percent Strategy Three, and 5 percent some other strategy."

The fact that lessons are the unit of study is also important for the value of the case reports. The lesson is a unit that has ecological validity for teachers. Lessons are the smallest unit that maintains the complex and systemic properties of teaching. Quality instruction cannot be described with a list of features: there is no feature (be it real-world problems, concrete representations, or any other) that is always beneficial. Which features are the right ones depends on the context, and the context is the lesson in which the features are embedded. Lessons also are linked directly with the curriculum that teachers are using to guide instruction. This linkage, more than anything else, makes the results of lesson study of immediate interest to other teachers using the same curriculum. It is why lesson study is so powerful in Japan, where there exist specific national goals for each course of study, and it is why we believe that if lesson study is to succeed in the United States, it will be implemented within school districts that have adopted a comprehensive and common curriculum.

Accumulating Knowledge About Teaching

The kind of knowledge produced by lesson-study groups is quite different from that traditionally produced by education researchers. Traditional research results are first validated in studies, then communicated in research journals to educators, who must then figure out how they apply to the classroom. The kind of knowledge produced by lesson study is accumulated in a different way. Because lesson study is carried out in classrooms, the problem of applying the findings to classrooms disappears. The application is direct and obvious. But we cannot immediately know how generalizable lesson-study results are across different teachers, schools, and children.

The fact that lessons linked with curricula are sharable, however, gives us a means of assessing the generality of findings. A first test concerns the ease with which lessons can be shared when they are passed through the filter of language. If teachers can describe lessons to other teachers in sufficient detail so that the other teachers can actually use the lessons, we can be fairly certain that both groups understand the essential characteristics of the lesson. Lessons that work across diverse groups of teachers can be said to generalize simply because they can be replicated.

The Role of Technology

The process of accumulating knowledge about teaching will be greatly enhanced by technology. The most useful information that can be shared about teaching includes examples of classroom lessons linked to evolving theoretical understandings of teaching. Instead of describing these lesson examples with reports such as those that Japanese teachers write, imagine if we could store them in large digital libraries that could link together video, audio, images of student work, and commentary by researchers and others into a single integrated database.

It is now possible to store video examples and related data on video servers that can be accessed over the internet and thus be physically located anywhere in the world. Curriculum developers, for example, could establish large archives of lessons that are organized around the specific structures of their curricula. Teacher groups could work on perfecting lessons, then post the results of their study, including a complete video record, on these large servers. Other teacher groups could access these archives in order to inform their own efforts to improve teaching. They could study archived lessons and actually collaborate interactively over the internet with the teachers who produced the lessons. The resulting discussions could be directly linked with concrete video examples, and over time such discussions would lead to development of a shared language for describing teaching—the way it is and the way it could be.

We want to emphasize that these distributed databases would not be just collections of lessons that teachers could download and use. In fact, many such libraries of model lessons are already being developed. What we are proposing is far more complex and far more powerful. The goal of studying these lessons would not be to copy them but, instead, to use them as examples from which new theories of teaching can be constructed. For, in our view, the professional teacher is not someone who simply copies what others have done but is, rather, one who reflects on and improves on what others have done, working to understand the basis of these improvements.

Building a national infrastructure for accumulating and sharing knowledge about teaching is something that should be done by the federal government in collaboration with curriculum developers and textbook publishers. When a plane crashes, the investigation is not left to local authorities. The reason for this is clear: The public has too much at stake to not allow everyone to learn from every crash. When problems are discovered, they are widely shared, together with possible solutions, so as to prevent more disasters from happening. The same attention must be paid to knowledge about teaching. Students are too precious to be guinea pigs for teachers forced to learn by themselves on the job. Creating knowledge that can be used, and then sharing that knowledge with each new generation of teachers, should be a high priority of our national education authorities.

Conclusion

In a book on teaching, it might be surprising that we have not recommended a particular way to teach. Instead, we have proposed the establishment of a national research-and-development system for the improvement of classroom teaching. Improving teaching, as we have said, is a cultural change and thus must happen in small steps. In the same way, building the kind of system we have proposed requires that we change the ways that teachers learn, which is also a cultural activity. This, too, will change slowly and in small steps. But that is not a bad thing. The system we have proposed is both modular and scalable. It can happen one district at a time and can evolve over many years. The important thing is that the system we are proposing is one that we desperately need if we are to look back a hundred years from now and recognize a history of gradual progress in improving teaching.

Although constructing this system will be difficult, it should cause some current problems with educational reform to diminish.

Take, for example, the highly charged political battles that are now being fought in California and elsewhere about the kind of mathematics instruction our children should be exposed to in school. Our earlier analyses of how policy affects practice reveal that regardless of who wins these battles, there is a good chance that little of any substance will change inside classrooms. But more to the point, the system we are proposing leaves the question of how best to teach up to the system itself to resolve, over time, through careful experimentation and study. Public debate is the only way to decide on the goals that will guide our educational system. But once the goals are decided, the best way we can help improve our children's education is not to continue taking sides on these explosive issues but to fight to institute some mechanism for improvement.

Progress will be slow. For the sake of the children we can hasten the start toward better teaching by taking the first step toward the process of continual improvement. But that quick step is only the beginning of a long journey.

CHAPTER 10

The True Profession of Teaching

T HE SYSTEM FOR improving teaching that we have just
presented challenges school districts, school boards,
superintendents, principals, and parents to undertake a
new, long-term process of improvement, but it places primary
responsibility for the process squarely on teachers. The success of the system depends on teachers' initiative, creativity,
and professional commitment. Some would question whether
teachers are up to the task, whether they can be handed the job
of improving their own teaching. There is, in our society, a
widespread lack of confidence in teachers.[1] When students'
achievement scores are below expectations, and when stories
of students' failures fill the media, teachers often are blamed
for the problems. More than that, they are ignored when we
look for solutions. Rather than turning to teachers for leadership and guidance, we look to business executives, to political
leaders, or to so-called educational experts for the answers.
Given this lack of trust, it is no wonder that, as we noted in

Chapter 1, the current reforms leave teaching almost completely out of the equation.

The lack of confidence in teachers is not limited to public and political communities. Even educators display a certain skepticism of teachers' inclination or ability to improve teaching.[2] Over the years, curriculum developers often have tried to create "teacher-proof" curricula—content that is to be presented to students in such a straightforward way that it could not be distorted by incompetent teachers.[3] There is also a long-standing degree of distrust between administrators and teachers, illustrated by the fact that principals usually observe teachers only when it is time to evaluate them. Teachers, in turn, take a very suspicious view of being observed.[4] This mistrust ruins one of teachers' richest learning opportunities—the opportunity to observe the practice of others and be observed yourself.

A Popular Solution: Professionalize Teachers

The perception that teachers are not up to the task of improving teaching and solving the country's educational problems is often captured in one short phrase: "Teachers are not professionals." To combat this attack, some defenders have launched a counteroffensive. Teachers, they say, are unfairly blamed for students' failures. It is not the teachers' fault that students perform poorly or learn less than we expect. Poverty, demographic changes, an erosion of traditional values, and a breakdown of supportive families are among the real causes,[5] yet society unfairly targets teachers because teaching has not been granted the status of other professions, like medicine or law or business. Society thinks that anyone can be a teacher, that little expertise is required. Because teachers are not fully appreciated for what they do, they are vulnerable to public attacks. To solve this problem, say their defenders, society should demand that teachers be given higher status and be treated as real professionals.

There are many ideas about how to turn teachers into high-status professionals: increased pay, increased certification requirements, more accountability, career ladders, peer review, training teachers as researchers, and encouraging teachers themselves to set the standards for entrance into their profession.[6] Not all of these stratagems are proposed by teachers' advocates, but they do have one thing in common: They presume that attributing to teachers the characteristics common to professionals in other fields will bring higher status and respect.

We believe, however, that attacking the problem simply by arbitrarily assigning professional characteristics to teachers mistakes the trappings for the profession. In fact, a profession is created not by certificates and censures but by the existence of a substantive body of professional knowledge, as well as a mechanism for improving it, and by the genuine desire of the profession's members to improve their practice.

Redefining the Problem

If the desire to improve is a key to build a true profession, then what is standing in the way? Some would say the answer is obvious—teachers do not have this desire, or at least they have not shown it. After all, teachers have not changed the way they teach for almost a century.[7] They continue teaching in traditional ways despite regular waves of educational reform. But before condemning teachers, consider what we have learned about teaching in the previous chapters. We can now see that most of our nation's problems with teaching arise from the script for teaching that has evolved in this country and from the absence of a mechanism for changing it.

The TIMSS videotapes show most American teachers teaching in much the same way—true to the American script. Many factors—students, parents, administrators, school structure, and more—maintain this cultural script, keep it in place, and discourage teachers from questioning it. The perception that they are unable to improve is premature at best; it is wrongheaded and destructive at worst.

Suppose teachers really do wish to improve how they teach. What can they do? Under normal circumstances, they can become better at using the teaching script they already have learned. But without some new ways of examining teaching, they are unlikely to identify alternatives that could improve students' learning even more. The environments in which most teachers work have been structured in ways that actually work against the kind of sustained collaboration that we have suggested is needed for significant and steady improvement.[8] So instead of assuming that teachers do not want to improve, we take a different view. We believe that the real problem lies in the teaching, not the teachers, and in the absence of resources available to help teachers improve how they teach.

How Did We Get to This Point?

Why is it that we in the United States have for so long accepted a script for teaching that might be inadequate, and why is there no system for improvement? An interesting turn of events in the early 1900s provides some insights into the problem. John Dewey, noted educator and philosopher, had shaped the laboratory school at the University of Chicago into a hotbed of educational improvement. This one school became a microcosm of the system we outlined in Chapters 8 and 9. Teachers and researchers, through collaborative planning and experimenting, developed knowledge of effective classroom practice and fed this knowledge back into the system. The lines between teachers and researchers were blurred; all were engaged in learning about teaching and how to improve it in the context of real classrooms.

But then things changed. Dewey left Chicago, and Charles Judd, Dewey's replacement, proposed a new method of improvement, one designed to bring the prestige and rigor of science to education. Central to Judd's approach was a distinction between scientists or researchers, who develop the best ideas, and teachers, who apply them. Judd was not alone. Many experts, including researchers such as Edward Thorndike, were impressed with the advances in science and wished to make education more scientific. The way to do this, they said, was to divide the labor: Researchers would discover the best methods and teachers would implement them in classrooms.

Over time, the views of Judd and others won the day. Research became a specially designated activity, distinct from teaching, and researchers became differentiated from classroom teachers. They even located themselves in different places—researchers moved to universities, and teachers stayed in schools.[9]

The same distinction between research and practice continues today, perhaps even more strongly. A large gulf separates researchers and classroom teachers.[10] Researchers work on better ways to teach and then hope that their findings will be applied by classroom teachers. We have pointed out in earlier chapters that this process has had little effect on standard teaching practice.

Because of the high status usually assigned to acquiring knowledge and the low status assigned to applying it, this distinction strongly reinforces the low professional status of teachers. And this is a distinction created and sustained *within* the educational community!

What is most damaging about the distinction, however, is that it prevents our country from implementing a system, sustained by teachers, for improving teaching. By hanging on to the research/teaching distinction, the educational world has robbed teachers of the opportunity to participate in the development of new knowledge about teaching. The U.S. educational establishment has been unable to envision a system that gives teachers the freedom and the responsibility to acquire *and* apply the knowledge needed to improve teaching over the long run. What is tragic about this is that there are no real alternatives. Teachers *must* be at the heart of the solution. Not only are they the gatekeepers for all improvement efforts, they are also in the best position to acquire the knowledge that is needed. They are, after all, the only ones who can improve teaching. Proposals that do not recognize this basic truth cannot succeed.

Clearly, blaming teachers for not improving teaching is unfair. It is unfair because, in fact, teachers have been encouraged, simply by virtue of their membership in our culture, to teach the way they do. It is unfair because they have been provided no system in which they might spend time and energy studying and improving teaching. But solving these problems does not require high-pitched rhetoric and protestations by defenders of teachers, claiming for them higher professional status. In fact, solving the problem of improving teaching requires shifting the focus from teach*ers* to teach*ing*. Instead of worrying about professionalizing teachers, we must think about what is required to professionalize teaching.

A Lasting Solution: Professionalize Teaching

As we noted in Chapter 8, a common American view of the classroom says that good teaching is an individual trait. Change the teacher, and the quality of teaching changes. Some teachers are effective and some are not, so the way to improve teaching is to recruit better teachers. But this perspective ignores a central truth about teaching: If the method is limited, students' learning will be limited no matter how talented the teacher. Teachers are only as good as the methods of teaching they use.

Because of America's focus on teach*ers,* we tend to look to individual innovators for signs of improvement. Because the usual methods of teaching are recognized as uninspiring, we look to individuals who have figured out clever ways around these standard methods. We shine spotlights on the unusual, the variations from standard practice. These heroic individual teachers stand out from the crowd and are applauded by reformers for innovation and creativity. They are given special awards. The standard, routine way of teaching is treated as just routine.

Celebrating individual innovations is fine, but individual innovations will never improve teaching in the average classroom. They cannot do so because they do not change *standard* practice. And if we hope to improve the practice of the profession, it is the standard, common practice that must improve. Sporadic end runs around the standard methods are not the answer; what is required is a steady, continuing effort to gradually improve the standard ways in which we teach.

In true professions, standard practices hold the wisdom of

the profession. It is when the standard practices of teaching are improved that a profession begins to emerge. Some might worry that trying to improve standard practice limits teachers' individual creativity and spontaneity. But listen, again, to Albert Shanker as he testified before the U.S. House of Representatives' Committee on Economic and Educational Opportunities: "Doctors don't try to figure out a new technique or procedure for every patient who comes into their office; they begin by using the standard techniques and procedures based on the experience of many doctors over the years. Nobody considers this a way of doctor-proofing medicine, although they do have a name for the failure to use standard practices—it's *malpractice.* The standard practices that all doctors (and other professionals) use contain the wisdom of the profession."[11]

America's script of teaching, the repository of its standard practices, has remained unexamined for too long. Teaching has not improved in this country because educators and parents have not provided a way for teachers to improve the script they use. It is time to begin building a research-and-development system like the one outlined in Chapters 8 and 9 to enable teachers to study teaching and to begin the long, steady process of improving the standard practice of the profession.

Perhaps it is ironic that professional status for teachers will come only when the focus shifts away from teachers and onto teaching. But that is what is required. When teachers have a way to act on their desire to improve, when they can point to increases in students' learning over time, and when they can disseminate into standard practice the improvements in teaching that are responsible, teaching will be on its way to becoming a true profession. And when teaching becomes a profession, teachers will inherit the professional badges that come from being members.

A Story from the Past

Our belief that teaching can become a true profession in the United States is bolstered by the fact that it has, at times, been a profession. No, not across the entire country and not for all time, but in some places and for brief periods. When teachers have seized unusual opportunities and taken on the task of improving teaching in their school or district, remarkable things have happened. A compelling and instructive example is related by William Johnson.[12] At the turn of the century, the Baltimore city schools were in trouble. Physical conditions were deplorable, and the instructional methods used by many teachers were unenlightened, to say the least. Joseph Mayer Rice, an informed observer of America's schools, published a series of articles in 1892 that focused on the conditions of schools in America's cities. The first article was titled "Evils in Baltimore."

But a group of Baltimore teachers, interested in improving classroom practices, convinced the Baltimore city public schools teachers' association to lobby the city school commissioners for time to meet and work together to improve teaching and learning in their classrooms. They wanted one afternoon each month to meet with other teachers. Teachers around the city who taught the same grade met to discuss methods of teaching that would facilitate improved student learning. Discussions centered on common problems of classroom practice. Wishing to share their insights and progress more widely, the city teachers began publishing a regular newsletter, *The Expert Pedagogue,* which was filled with suggestions for improved teaching.

After several years of teacher meetings and newsletter publication, the district made an administrative decision that was to have a fatal impact on the burgeoning profession of teaching in Baltimore. In 1900, a new superintendent was hired. Eager to bring new, progressive ideas into the district, the superintendent reorganized the form of in-service education. The monthly meetings of teachers were replaced with presentations by educational experts. The presentations, given weekly and after hours, were mostly demonstrations of model lessons developed by the "experts." Having no forum for continuing collaboration, the teachers' newsletter soon disappeared; arising in its place was the *Maryland Educational Journal,* produced by experts to promote progressive practices. Teachers were back in their role of trying to implement the recommendations of others. Business had returned to normal. William Johnson summarized this story by noting the irony: Teachers in Baltimore had begun the long journey to improve classroom practice and to professionalize teaching. The new superintendent entered with the same goals, but, not recognizing the central role that teachers must play in this process, he squelched the very movement he was trying to build. For a brief moment, however, teaching in the Baltimore schools had been on its way to becoming a true profession.

This story of what happened in Baltimore, along with the stories of what is happening now in a number of schools and districts scattered around the country, shows that building a profession of teaching in the United States is not an impossible dream.[13] But it will take commitment—and a vision.

A Vision of the Future

The star teachers of the twentieth century have been those who broke away from the crowd and created different and unusual methods of teaching. They distinguished themselves by being different, by leaving the standard practice behind.

They gained fame by rising above the routine and showing the effectiveness of alternative forms of teaching. Although these efforts won the applause of educational critics, they did not have much effect on standard practice.

The star teachers of the twenty-first century will be those who work together to infuse the best ideas into standard practice. They will be teachers who collaborate to build a system that has the goal of improving students' learning in the "average" classroom, who work to gradually improve standard classroom practices. In a true profession, the wisdom of the profession's members finds its way into the most common methods. The best that we know becomes the standard way of doing something. The star teachers of the twenty-first century will be teachers who work every day to improve teaching—not only their own but that of the whole profession.

Notes

PREFACE

1. Husen, T. (1967). *International study of achievement in mathematics.* New York: Wiley; McKnight, C. C.; Crosswhite, F. J.; Dossey, J. A.; Kifer, E.; Swafford, J. O.; Travers, K. J.; and Cooney, T. J. (1987). *The underachieving curriculum: Assessing U.S. school mathematics from an international perspective.* Champaign, Ill.: Stipes.

CHAPTER 1: THE TEACHING GAP

1. On October 27, 1998, President Clinton signed into law the Labor, Health, and Human Services bill, which provided $1.2 billion to help local school districts hire and pay the salaries and benefits of more than 30,000 additional teachers. The funds are a down payment on the president's plan to hire 100,000 new teachers over seven years to reduce class size in grades one to three to a national average of eighteen. For details on the Class Size Initiative, see http://www.ed.gov/PressReleases/10-1998/class.html.

2. Ample evidence exists to show that most reform efforts rarely change fundamentally what happens inside classrooms. For example: Cuban, L. (1993). *How teachers taught: Constancy and change in American classrooms, 1890–1990,* 2nd ed. New York: Teachers College Press; *Educational Evaluation and Policy Analysis* (1990). Vol. 12, No. 3 [special issue]; Griffin, G. A. (1995). Influences of shared decision making on school and classroom

activity: Conversations with five teachers. *Elementary School Journal* 96, 29–45; Stake, R., and Easley, J. (eds.). (1978). *Case studies in science education.* Urbana, Ill.: University of Illinois; Tyack, D., and Cuban, L. (1995). *Tinkering toward utopia: A century of public school reform.* Cambridge, Mass.: Harvard University Press.

3. Bruner, J. (1996). *The culture of education.* Cambridge, Mass.: Harvard University Press. P. 86.

4. Berliner, D. C., and Biddle, B. J. (1995). *The manufactured crisis: Myths, frauds, and the attack on America's public schools.* New York: Addison Wesley; Reynolds, A. J., and Walberg, H. J. (1992). A process model of mathematics achievement and attitude. *Journal for Research in Mathematics Education* 23, 306–28.

5. Slavin, R. E. (1996). Reforming state and federal policies to support adoption of proven practice. *Education Researcher* 25 (9), 4–5 (p. 4).

6. Berliner, D. C., and Biddle, B. J. (1995). *The manufactured crisis: Myths, frauds, and the attack on America's public schools.* New York: Addison Wesley; Hirsch, E. D. Jr. (1996). *The schools we need: And why we don't have them.* New York: Doubleday.

7. Wearne, D., and Kouba, V. L. (in press). Rational numbers. In E. A. Silver and P. A. Kenney (eds.), *Results from the seventh mathematics assessment of the National Assessment of Educational Progress.* Reston, Va.: National Council of Teachers of Mathematics. The relatively poor preparation of students in mathematics and science has real consequences. On September 24, 1998, the U.S. House of Representatives approved a bill allowing an additional 142,500 foreign skilled workers to enter the country, thus exempting them from normal immigration quotas. The bill was designed to meet the needs of high-technology industries that are unable to find adequate skilled workers among the U.S. population.

8. Stevenson, H. W., and Stigler, J. W. (1992). *The learning gap: Why our schools are failing and what we can learn from Japanese and Chinese education.* New York: Simon and Schuster.

9. Husen, T. (1967). *International study of achievement in mathematics.* New York: Wiley; McKnight, C. C.; Crosswhite, F. J.; Dossey,

J. A.; Kifer, E.; Swafford, J. O.; Travers, K. J.; and Cooney, T. J. (1987). *The underachieving curriculum: Assessing U.S. school mathematics from an international perspective.* Champaign, Ill.: Stipes.

10. National Center for Education Statistics. (1996). *Pursuing excellence: Initial findings from the Third International Mathematics and Science Study.* Washington, D.C.: U.S. Department of Education.

11. California Department of Education. (1987). *English–Language Arts framework for California public schools.* Sacramento: California Department of Education. (1992). *Mathematics framework for California public schools.* Sacramento: California Department of Education.

12. See, for example, an exchange in the *New York Times,* August 11, 1997, p. A19 ("Creative Math or Just Fuzzy Math"), and responding letters to the editor, August 17, 1997, p. E14.

CHAPTER 2: METHODS FOR STUDYING TEACHING IN GERMANY, JAPAN, AND THE UNITED STATES

1. Readers interested in more detailed descriptions of the full TIMSS study should consult http://nces.ed.gov/timss/publist.html.

2. A full description of the methods used in conducting the video study is beyond the scope of this book. Interested readers should consult Stigler, J. W.; Gonzales, P.; Kawanaka, T.; Knoll, S.; and Serrano, A. (1999). *The TIMSS videotape classroom study: Methods and findings from an exploratory research project on eighth grade mathematics instruction in Germany, Japan, and the United States.* Washington, D.C.: National Center for Education Statistics (www.ed.gov/NCES).

3. The original intent was to videotape one hundred classrooms in each country. The no-substitution rule eliminated nineteen classrooms in the United States, and the Japanese collaborators decided that fifty classrooms would be sufficient in their country because of its relatively small size and homogeneity.

CHAPTER 3: IMAGES OF TEACHING

1. All names, in this lesson and all the others reported in this chapter, are fictional; however, the correct gender is retained.

CHAPTER 4: REFINING THE IMAGES

1. Schmidt, W. H.; McKnight, C. C.; and Raizen, S. A. (1996). *A splintered vision: An investigation of U.S. science and mathematics education.* Boston: Kluwer Academic Publishers.

2. All cross-national differences reported in this chapter are supported by thorough statistical analyses. Interested readers should consult Stigler, J. W.; Gonzales, P.; Kawanaka, T.; Knoll, S.; and Serrano, A. (1999). *The TIMSS videotape classroom study: Methods and findings from an exploratory research project on eighth grade mathematics instruction in Germany, Japan, and the United States.* Washington, D.C.: National Center for Education Statistics (www.ed.gov/NCES).

3. National Center for Education Statistics. (1996). *Pursuing excellence: A study of U.S. eighth-grade mathematics and science teaching, learning, curriculum, and achievement in international context.* Washington, D.C.: U.S. Department of Education.

4. Several studies have shown that students identify and remember the major points of more coherent lessons better than those of less coherent lessons [Fernandez, C.; Yoshida, M.; and Stigler, J. W. (1992). Learning mathematics from classroom instruction: On relating lessons to pupils' interpretations. *Journal of the Learning Sciences* 2(4), 333–65. Yoshida, M.; Fernandez, C.; and Stigler, J. W. (1993). Japanese and American students' differential recognition memory for teachers' statements during a mathematics lesson. *Journal of Educational Psychology* 85, 610–17].

5. This conclusion matches precisely the one arrived at by looking directly at the curricula commonly used in each country [Schmidt, W. H.; McKnight, C. C.; and Raizen, S. A. (1996). *A splintered vision: An investigation of U.S. science and mathematics education.* Boston: Kluwer Academic Publishers].

6. The Math Group was led by Professor Alfred Manaster of the Uni-

versity of California at San Diego. Other members of the group were Wallace Etterbeek, Phillip Emig, and Barbara Wells. For additional analyses conducted by the Math Group, see Manaster, A. B. (1998). Some characteristics of eighth grade mathematics classes in the TIMSS videotape study. *American Mathematical Monthly, 105*, 793–805.

7. See, for example, Doyle, W. (1983). Academic work. *Review of Educational Research* 53, 159–99; Doyle, W. (1988). Work in mathematics classes: The context of students' thinking during instruction. *Educational Psychologist* 23, 167–80; Schoenfeld, A. H. (1985). *Mathematical problem solving.* Orlando, Fla.: Academic Press.

8. The importance of engaging in creative, inventive work has long been recognized as crucial for developing deep understanding [Piaget, J. (1973). *To understand is to invent.* New York: Grossman; Resnick, L. B. (1980). The role of invention in the development of mathematical competence. In R. H. Kluwe and H. Spada (eds.), *Developmental models of thinking.* New York: Academic Press, pp. 213–44] and the benefits of engaging students in analyzing multiple solution methods to mathematical problems are detailed in Hiebert, J., et al. (1997). *Making sense: Teaching and learning mathematics with understanding.* Portsmouth, N.H.: Heinemann.

CHAPTER 5: TEACHING IS A SYSTEM

1. Teachers in 57 percent of U.S. lessons used the overhead projector, in 67 percent, the chalkboard. In Japan, the percentages were 6 and 100, respectively. See Stigler, J. W.; Gonzales, P.; Kawanaka, T.; Knoll, S.; and Serrano, A. (1999). *The TIMSS videotape classroom study: Methods and findings from an exploratory research project on eighth grade mathematics instruction in Germany, Japan, and the United States.* Washington, D.C.: National Center for Education Statistics (www.ed.gov/NCES).

2. Japanese teachers also used something we called "posters": prepared statements of solution methods or principles that they attached to the chalkboard at critical points during the lesson to label students' work (which they apparently anticipated) or to summarize major ideas. Posters are fully consistent with a system

in which visual aids provide records of instructional tasks, solution methods, and major ideas.

3. See, for example, Cuban, L. (1993). *How teachers taught: Constancy and change in American classrooms, 1890–1990,* 2nd ed. New York: Teachers College Press; Fey, J. (1979). Mathematics teaching today: Perspectives from three national surveys. *Mathematics Teacher* 72, 490–504; Hoetker, J., and Ahlbrand, W. P., Jr. (1969). The persistence of the recitation. *American Educational Research Journal* 6, 145–67; Sirotnik, K. A. (1983). What you see is what you get—consistency, persistency, and mediocrity in classrooms. *Harvard Educational Review* 53, 16–31.

4. Lortie, D. C. (1975). *Schoolteacher: A sociological study.* Chicago: University of Chicago Press; Wideen, M.; Mayer-Smith, J.; and Moon, B. (1998). A critical analysis of the research on learning to teach: Making the case for an ecological perspective on inquiry. *Review of Educational Research* 68, 130–78; Nemser, S. F. (1983). Learning to teach. In L. Shulman & G. Sykes (eds.), *Handbook of teaching and policy.* New York: Longman. Pp. 150–70.

CHAPTER 6: TEACHING IS A CULTURAL ACTIVITY

1. Ronald Gallimore makes many of these same points in "Classrooms are just another cultural activity." In D. L. Speece and B. K. Keogh (eds.). (1996). *Research on classroom ecologies: Implications for inclusion of children with learning disabilities.* Mahwah, N.J.: Erlbaum. Pp. 229–50. The origins of these ideas can be traced to earlier writings, such as Cazden, C.; John, V.; and Hymes, D. (eds.). (1972). *Functions of language in the classroom.* New York: Teachers College Press.

2. The same categories of core beliefs have been suggested by other researchers. See, for example, Griffin, S., and Case, R. (1997). Rethinking the primary school math curriculum: An approach based on cognitive science. *Issues in Education* 3(1), 1–49; Thompson, A. G. (1992). Teachers' beliefs and conceptions: A synthesis of research. In D. A. Grouws (ed.), *Handbook of research on mathematics teaching and learning.* New York: Macmillan. Pp. 127–46.

3. There is a strong American tradition in behaviorist psychology, a psychology that addresses most directly issues of skill learning. Behaviorism, or connectionism, was developed most fully by E. L. Thorndike in the early 1900s and elaborated in different ways by B. F. Skinner and R. M. Gagne.

4. The psychology of learning that underlies this approach is familiar in the United States but is not the psychology that has taken hold in everyday teaching in the United States. See, for example, the writings of J. Dewey and J. Piaget and numerous recent works that have elaborated these ideas.

5. *Kyoshiyo shidosho: Shogakko sansu 5 nen (Teacher's guidebook: Elementary mathematics 5th grade).* (1991). Tokyo: Gakkotosho.

6. One item on the questionnaire given to U.S. eighth-grade mathematics teachers in the TIMSS sample asked them to select, among sixteen choices, those that limited their effectiveness in the classroom. The second most frequent choice, just behind lack of student interest, was the range of abilities among students in the same class (selected by 45 percent of the respondents). See also a survey of its members by the American Federation of Teachers, reported in the Spring 1996 (Vol. 20, No. 1) issue of *American Educator,* pp. 18–21.

7. See the following article for an analysis of how the variety of student responses in a Japanese classroom benefits the whole class: Hatano, G., and Inagaki, K. (1991). Sharing cognition through collective comprehension activity. In L. B. Resnick, J. M. Levine, and S. D. Teasley (eds.), *Perspectives on socially shared cognition.* Washington, D.C.: APA. Pp. 331–48.

8. Sasaki, Akira. (1997). *Jugyo kenkyu no kadai to jissen (Issues and implementation of lesson study).* Tokyo: Kioiku Kaihatsu Kenkyujo.

9. A common reform approach in the United States is to try to reform mathematics instruction by adding more features, such as concrete materials or problem solving. Many experts think that the indicators provide the road map we need to improve. See, for example, Stedman, L. C. (1997). International achievement differences: An assessment of a new perspective. *Educational Researcher* 26 (3), 4–15. After reviewing a few teaching indicators from an earlier

international study, Stedman concludes: "These descriptions of our pedagogical weaknesses are compelling and provide clear directions for reforming our teaching and curricula" (p. 11).

10. Cohen, D. (1996). Standards-based school reform: Policy, practice, and performance. In H. F. Ladd (ed.), *Holding schools accountable: Performance-based reform in education.* Washington, D.C.: Brookings Institution; Guthrie, J. W. (ed.). (1990). *Educational Evaluation and Policy Analysis* 12 (3), special issue.

11. Bosse, M. J. (1995). The NCTM Standards in light of the new math movement: A warning! *Journal of Mathematical Behavior* 14, 177–201; DeVault, M. V., and Weaver, J. F. (1970). Forces and issues related to curriculum and instruction, K–6. In P. S. Jones (ed.), *A history of mathematics education in the United States and Canada: Thirty-second yearbook.* Washington, D.C.: National Council of Teachers of Mathematics. Pp. 93–152; Osborne, A. R., and Crosswhite, F. J. (1970). Forces and issues related to curriculum and instruction, 7–12. In Jones, *A history of mathematics education in the United States and Canada.* Pp. 155–297.

12. Freeman, D. J., and Porter, A. C. (1989). Do textbooks dictate the content of mathematics instruction in elementary schools? *American Educational Research Journal* 26, 403–21; Stodolsky, S. (1988). *The subject matters: Classroom activity in math and social studies.* Chicago: University of Chicago Press.

13. Conference Board of the Mathematical Sciences. (1975). *Overview and analysis of school mathematics, K–12.* Washington, D.C.: Conference Board of the Mathematical Sciences. The quote was taken from p. 77.

14. Leinhardt, G. (1993). On teaching. In R. Glaser (ed.), *Advances in instructional psychology,* Vol. 4. Hillsdale, N.J.: Erlbaum. Pp. 1–54. Even the most visible and well-intentioned reforms can be misinterpreted as single-feature changes: McLeod, D. B.; Stake, R. E.; Schappelle, B.; Mellissinos, M.; and Gierl, M. J. (1996). Setting the Standards: NCTM's role in the reform of mathematics education. In S. A. Raizen and E. D. Britton (eds.). *Bold ventures,* Vol. 3: *Case studies of U.S. innovations in science and mathematics education.* Dordrecht: Kluwer. Pp. 13–132.

15. Saxe, G. B.; Gearhart, M.; and Dawson, V. (1996). *When can educational reforms make a difference? The influence of curriculum and teacher professional development programs on children's understanding fractions.* Unpublished paper.

CHAPTER 7: BEYOND REFORM: JAPAN'S APPROACH TO THE IMPROVEMENT OF CLASSROOM TEACHING

1. Most efforts that have focused on improving teaching in a systematic way have been relatively small-scale, experimental efforts that have not gained national prominence outside the research community. With respect to mathematics teaching, see, for example, Fennema, E.; Carpenter, T. P.; and Peterson, P. L. (1989). Learning mathematics with understanding: Cognitively guided instruction. In J. E. Brophy (ed.), *Advances in research on teaching,* Vol. 1. Greenwich, Conn.: JAI Press, pp. 195–221; and Schifter, D., and Fosnot, C. T. (1993). *Reconstructing mathematics education: Stories of teachers meeting the challenge of reform.* New York: Teachers College Press. The effort of the National Council of Teachers of Mathematics that we describe here is somewhat unique in its high visibility, at least within the educational community.

2. National Council of Teachers of Mathematics. (1991). *Professional standards for teaching mathematics.* Reston, Va.: National Council of Teachers of Mathematics.

3. Albert Shanker told this story at a Pew Forum meeting in Jackson Hole, Wyoming, in July 1996. It was reprinted in a special issue of the *American Educator,* Spring/Summer 1997, Vol. 21, Nos. 1 and 2, p. 37.

4. *Educational Evaluation and Policy Analysis,* Vol. 12, No. 3. (1990); Saxe, G. B.; Gearhart, M.; and Dawson, V. (1996). *When can educational reforms make a difference? The influence of curriculum and teacher professional development programs on children's understanding of fractions.* Unpublished paper; McLeod, D. B.; Stake, R. E.; Schappelle, B.; Mellissinos, M.; and Gierl, M. J. (1996). Setting the Standards: NCTM's role in the reform of mathematics edu-

cation. In S. A. Raizen and E. D. Britton (eds.). *Bold ventures,* Vol. 3: *Case studies of U.S. innovations in science and mathematics education.* Dordrecht: Kluwer. Pp. 13–132.

5. Lewis, C., and Tsuchida, I. (1997). Planned educational change in Japan: The shift to student-centered elementary science. *Journal of Educational Policy* 12, 313–31.

6. Shimahara, N. K. (1997). *Educational reforms in Japan and the United States: Implications for civic education.* Paper presented at the annual meeting of the Educational Research Association of Singapore, Singapore.

7. Fewer high schools appear to engage in formalized *kounaiken-shuu;* teacher development tends to be more idiosyncratic and to vary more from school to school. This is probably due, in part, to the departmental specialization of high schools and to the pressures imposed by entrance exam preparations [see Yoshida, M. (1999). *Lesson study: An ethnographic investigation of school-based teacher development in Japan.* Doctoral dissertation, University of Chicago.]

8. Takemura, S., and Shimizu, K. (1993). Goals and strategies for science teaching as perceived by elementary teachers in Japan and the United States. *Peabody Journal of Education* 68 (4), 23–33; Shimahara, N. K., and Sakai, A. (1995). *Learning to teach in two cultures: Japan and the United States.* New York: Garland.

9. Lewis, C., and Tsuchida, I. (1997). Planned educational change in Japan: The shift to student-centered elementary science. *Journal of Educational Policy* 12, 313–31.

10. Lewis, C., and Tsuchida, I. (1997). Planned educational change in Japan: The shift to student-centered elementary science. *Journal of Educational Policy* 12, 313–31; Lewis, C., and Tsuchida, I. (1998). A lesson is like a swiftly flowing river: How research lessons improve Japanese education. *American Educator,* 22 (4), 12–17, 50–52; Shimahara, N. K. (1998). The Japanese model of professional development: Teaching as a craft. *Teaching and Teacher Education,* 14, 451–62; Shimahara, N. K., and Sakai, A. (1995). *Learning to teach in two cultures: Japan and the United States.* New York: Garland; Yoshida, M. (1999). *Lesson study: An*

ethnographic investigation of school-based teacher development in Japan. Doctoral dissertation, University of Chicago. Special issue of the *Peabody Journal of Education* 1993, Vol. 68, No. 4.

11. Orihara, Kazuo (ed.). (1993). *Shogakko: Kenkyu Jugyo no susume kata mikata* (*Elementary school: Implementing and observing research lessons*). Tokyo: Bunkyo-shoin.

12. Descriptions of the common professional development opportunities for American teachers can be found in Cohen, D. K., and Hill, H. C. (1998). *Instructional policy and classroom performance: The mathematics reform in California.* Ann Arbor: University of Michigan; Lubeck, S. Teachers and the teaching profession in the United States. In *The education system in the United States: Case study findings,* draft vol. Ann Arbor: University of Michigan Center for Human Growth and Development. Pp. 241–318; Weiss, I. (1994). *A profile of science and mathematics education in the United States: 1993.* Chapel Hill, N.C.: Horizon Research, Inc. There are, however, some local schools and districts where teachers have been given much richer opportunities to improve teaching. See, for example, Cognition and Technology Group at Vanderbilt. (1997). *The Jasper project: Lessons in curriculum, instruction, assessment, and professional development.* Mahwah, N.J.: Erlbaum; Elmore, R. F.; Peterson, P. L.; and McCarthey, S. J. (1996). *Restructuring in the classroom: Teaching, learning, and school organization.* San Francisco: Jossey-Bass; Franke, M. L.; Carpenter, T. P.; Fennema, E.; Ansell, E.; and Behrend, J. (1998). Understanding teachers' self-sustaining, generative change in the context of professional development. *Teaching and Teacher Education* 14(1), 67–80; Stein, M. K.; Silver, E. A; and Smith, M. S. (1998). Mathematics reform and teacher development: A community of practice perspective. In J. Greeno and S. Goldman (eds.), *Thinking practices in mathematics and science learning.* Mahwah, N.J.: Erlbaum; and Swafford, J. O.; Jones, G. A.; and Thornton, C. A. (1997). Increased knowledge in geometry and instructional practice. *Journal for Research in Mathematics Education* 28, 467–83. It is interesting that the activities described in these reports share many features with Japanese lesson study. It also is the case that successful teaching-improvement programs in other countries contain some of these elements. See, for example, Paine, L., and Ma, L. (1994).

Teachers working together: A dialogue on organizational and cultural perspectives of Chinese teachers. *International Journal of Educational Research* 19 (8), 675–98.

13. Gallimore, R. (1996). Classrooms are just another cultural activity. In D. L. Speece and B. K. Keogh (eds.), *Research on classroom ecologies: Implications for inclusion of children with learning disabilities.* Mahwah, N.J.: Erlbaum. Pp. 229–50. Quote taken from p. 232.

14. Lortie, D. C. (1975). *Schoolteacher: A sociological study.* Chicago: University of Chicago Press.

15. Lewis, C. C. (December 1997). *Improving Japanese science education: How "research lessons" build teachers, schools, and a national curriculum.* Paper presented at the Conference on Mathematics and Elementary Science Education, Berlin, Germany. P. 13.

16. Lewis, C. C. (December 1997). *Improving Japanese science education: How "research lessons" build teachers, schools, and a national curriculum.* Paper presented at the Conference on Mathematics and Elementary Science Education, Berlin, Germany.

17. Lewis, C. C. (December 1997). *Improving Japanese science education: How "research lessons" build teachers schools, and a national curriculum.* Paper presented at the Conference on Mathematics and Elementary Science Education, Berlin, Germany. P. 3.

CHAPTER 8: SETTING THE STAGE
FOR CONTINUOUS IMPROVEMENT

1. Tyack, D., and Cuban, L. (1995). *Tinkering toward utopia: A century of public school reform.* Cambridge, Mass.: Harvard University Press.

2. Gallimore, R. (1996). Classrooms are just another cultural activity. In D. L. Speece and B. K. Keogh (eds.), *Research on classroom ecologies: Implications for inclusion of children with learning disabilities.* Mahwah, N.J.: Erlbaum. Pp. 229–50.

3. Joyce, B.; Wolf, J.; and Calhoun, E. (1993). *The self-renewing school.* Alexandria, Va.: Association for Supervision and Curriculum Development. Quote taken from p. 20.

4. Joyce, B.; Wolf, J.; and Calhoun, E. (1993). *The self-renewing school.* Alexandria, Va.: Association for Supervision and Curriculum Development. Quote taken from p. 19.

5. Carnegie Forum on Education and the Economy. (1986). *A nation prepared: Teachers for the twenty-first century.* Washington, D.C.: Carnegie Forum on Education and the Economy; Holmes Group. (1986). *Tomorrow's teachers: A report of the Holmes Group.* East Lansing, Mich.: Holmes Group; National Board for Professional Teaching Standards. (1996). *Guide to National Board certification.* Princeton, N.J.: Educational Testing Service.

6. Anderson, J. R.; Reder, L. M.; and Simon, H. A. (1996). Situated learning and education. *Educational Researcher* 25 (4), 5–11; Greeno, J. G. (1997). On claims that answer the wrong questions. *Educational Researcher* 26 (1), 5–17; Lave, J. (1988). *Cognition in practice.* New York: Cambridge University Press; Marsick, V. J. (1998). Transformative learning from experience in the knowledge era. *Daedalus,* 127 (4), 119–36.

7. Eisner, E. W. (1979). *The educational imagination: On the design and evaluation of school programs.* New York: Macmillan; Sarason, S. B. (1983). *Schooling in America: Scapegoat and salvation.* New York: Free Press; Schaefer, R. J. (1967). *The school as a center of inquiry.* New York: Harper and Row; Tharp, R. G., and Gallimore, R. (1988). *Rousing minds to life: Teaching, learning, and schooling in social context.* Cambridge, England: Cambridge University Press; Cohen, D. K., and Hill, H. C. (1998). *Instructional policy and classroom performance: The mathematics reform in California.* Ann Arbor: University of Michigan; Lubeck, S. (1996). Teachers and the teaching profession in the United States. In *The education system in the United States: Case study findings* (draft volume). Ann Arbor: University of Michigan Center for Human Growth and Development. Pp. 241–318.

8. Numerous research reports have turned this claim into one of the most well-supported conclusions in the literature on educational improvement. See, for example, an early study by J. W. Little (1982). Norms of collegiality and experimentation: Workplace conditions of school success. *American Educational Research Journal* 19, 325–40; and a recent review by L. Darling-Hammond (1998).

Teachers and teaching: Testing policy hypotheses from a National Commission report. *Educational Researcher* 27 (1), 5–15.

9.   Elmore, R. F.; Peterson, P. L.; and McCarthey, S. J. (1996). *Restructuring in the classroom: Teaching, learning, and school organization.* San Francisco: Jossey-Bass; Stein, M. K.; Silver, E. A.; and Smith, M. S. (1998). Mathematics reform and teacher development: A community of practice perspective. In J. Greeno and S. Goldman (eds.), *Thinking practices in mathematics and science learning.* Mahwah, N.J.: Erlbaum; Tharp, R. G., and Gallimore, R. (1988). *Rousing minds to life: Teaching, learning, and schooling in social context.* Cambridge, England: Cambridge University Press.

10.   Elmore, R. (1996). Getting to scale with good educational practice. *Harvard Educational Review* 66, 1–26; Cohen, D. K., and Hill, H. C. (1998). *Instructional policy and classroom performance: The mathematics reform in California.* Ann Arbor: University of Michigan; Lubeck, S. (1996). Teachers and the teaching profession in the United States. In *The education system in the United States: Case study findings* (draft volume). Ann Arbor: University of Michigan Center for Human Growth and Development. Pp. 241–318.

11.   Glass, T. E. (1992). *The 1992 Study of the American School Superintendency: America's education leaders in a time of reform.* Arlington, Va: American Association of School Administrators.

12.   School boards are painted as ineffective by at least one recent study [Hess, F. (1998). *Spinning wheels.* Washington, D.C.: Brookings Institution]. But the survey of principals conducted as part of TIMSS showed that, in many districts, school boards have the final say in making many educational decisions and therefore are positioned to take an active leadership role.

13.   Cuban, L. (1993). *How teachers taught: Constancy and change in American classrooms, 1890–1990,* 2nd ed. New York: Teachers College Press; Elmore, R. F., and McLaughlin, M. W. (1988). *Steady work: Policy, practice, and the reform of American education.* Santa Monica, Calif.: Rand Corporation; Tyack, D., and Cuban, L. (1995). *Tinkering toward utopia: A century of public school reform.* Cambridge, Mass.: Harvard University Press.

14.   National Science Board. (1998). *Failing our children: Implications*

of the Third Mathematics and Science Study. Available on-line at http://www.nsf.gov/nsb/documents.

15. Cohen, D. K., and Barnes, C. A. (1993). Pedagogy and policy. In D. K. Cohen, M. W. McLaughlin, and J. E. Talbert (eds.), *Teaching for understanding: Challenges for policy and practice.* San Francisco: Jossey-Bass. Pp. 207–39.

16. Shanker, A. (1993). Where we stand: Ninety-two hours. *New York Times,* 24 January. Reprinted in *American Educator* 21 (1, 2), 1997, pp. 33–34.

17. Goldenberg, C. N., and Sullivan, J. (1994). *Making change happen in a language-minority school: A search for coherence* (EPR #13). Washington, D.C.: Center for Applied Linguistics; Elmore, R. F.; Peterson, P. L.; and McCarthey, S. J. (1996). *Restructuring in the classroom: Teaching, learning, and school organization.* San Francisco: Jossey-Bass; Stein, M. K.; Silver, E. A.; and Smith, M. S. (1998). Mathematics reform and teacher development: A community of practice perspective. In J. Greeno and S. Goldman (eds.), *Thinking practices in mathematics and science learning.* Mahwah, N.J.: Erlbaum.

18. One of the major findings from the case studies of TIMSS was the difference in the weekly work schedule of teachers in the United States, Germany, and Japan. U.S. teachers say that one of the biggest constraints on improving practice is the lack of professional time outside of their classrooms. Indeed, U.S. teachers have less scheduled time to meet and plan for instruction than their foreign colleagues. Increasing the time for this purpose is seen by some federal policymakers as one of the primary implications of these cross-cultural data [*Trying to beat the clock: Uses of professional time in three countries.* (1998). Washington, D.C.: U.S. Department of Education, Office of Policy and Planning].

19. Organization for Economic Cooperation and Development. (1995). *Education at a glance: OECD indicators.* Paris: Organization for Economic Cooperation and Development.

20. Darling-Hammond, L. (1997). *The right to learn.* San Francisco: Jossey-Bass.

21. A more in-depth analysis of alternative ways of restructuring teach-

ers' time can be found in *Trying to beat the clock: Uses of teacher professional time in three countries.* (1998). Washington, D.C.: U.S. Department of Education, Office of Policy and Planning.

22. Greenwald, R.; Hedges, L. V.; and Laine, R. D. (1996). The effect of school resources on student achievement. *Review of Educational Research* 66, 361–96.

CHAPTER 9: THE STEADY WORK
OF IMPROVING TEACHING

1. In their 1996 book, *Restructuring in the classroom: Teaching, learning, and school organization* (San Francisco: Jossey-Bass), R. Elmore, P. Peterson, and S. McCarthey report that some reform-minded schools used teachers' time in a way that improved classroom practice and other schools did not. Other studies also have shown that what teachers do with their professional development time makes a big difference [see, for example, Cohen, D. K., and Hill, H. C. (1998). *Instructional policy and classroom performance: The mathematics reform in California.* Ann Arbor: University of Michigan; and Griffin, G. A. (1995). Influences of shared decision making on school and classroom activity: Conversations with five teachers. *Elementary School Journal* 96, 29–45].

2. The phrase "steady work" was used by R. Elmore and M. McLaughlin in their 1988 book, *Steady work: Policy, practice, and the reform of American education.* We have in mind much the same meaning as they did—improving education is a long-term venture that requires continuing small improvements.

3. Brown, C. A.; Smith, M. S.; and Stein, M. K. (April 1996). *Linking teacher support to enhanced classroom instruction.* Paper presented at the annual meeting of the American Educational Research Association, New York; Cognition and Technology Group at Vanderbilt. (1997). *The Jasper project: Lessons in curriculum, instruction, assessment, and professional development.* Mahwah, N.J.: Erlbaum; Cohen, D. K.; McLaughlin, M. W.; and Talbert, J. E. (eds.). (1993). *Teaching for understanding: Challenges for policy and practice.* San Francisco: Jossey-Bass; Darling-Hammond, L. (1998). Teachers and

teaching: Testing policy hypotheses from a national commission report. *Educational Researcher* 27 (1), 5–15; Elmore, R. F.; Peterson, P. L.; and McCarthey, S. J. (1996). *Restructuring in the classroom: Teaching, learning, and school organization.* San Francisco: Jossey-Bass; Fennema, E.; Carpenter, T. P.; Franke, M. L.; Levi, L.; Jacobs, V. R.; and Empson, S. B. (1996). A longitudinal study of learning to use children's thinking in mathematics instruction. *Journal for Research in Mathematics Education* 27, 403–34; Franke, M. L.; Carpenter, T. P.; Fennema, E.; Ansell, E.; and Behrend, J. (1998). Understanding teachers' self-sustaining, generative change in the context of professional development. *Teaching and Teacher Education* 14 (1), 67–80; Little, J. W. (1982). Norms of collegiality and experimentation: Workplace conditions of school success. *American Educational Research Journal* 19, 325–40; Little, J. W. (1993). Teachers' professional development in a climate of educational reform. *Educational Evaluation and Policy Analysis* 15, 129–51; Schifter, D., and Fosnot, C. T. (1993). *Reconstructing mathematics education: Stories of teachers meeting the challenge of reform.* New York: Teachers College Press; Tharp, R. G., and Gallimore, R. (1988). *Rousing minds to life: Teaching, learning, and schooling in social context.* Cambridge, England: Cambridge University Press.

4. Burnaford, G.; Fischer, J.; and Hobson, D. (eds.). (1996). *Teachers doing research.* Mahwah, N.J.: Erlbaum; Cochran-Smith, M., and Lytle, S. L. (1990). Research on teaching and teacher research: The issues that divide. *Educational Researcher* 19 (2), 2–11; Cochran-Smith, M., and Lytle, S. L. (1993). *Inside/outside: Teacher research and knowledge.* New York: Teachers College Press; Franke, M. L.; Carpenter, T. P.; Fennema, E.; Ansell, E.; and Behrend, J. (1998). Understanding teachers' self-sustaining, generative change in the context of professional development. *Teaching and Teacher Education* 14(1), 67–80. Hollingsworth, S., and Sockett, H. (eds.). (1994). *Teacher research and educational reform: 93rd Yearbook of the Society for the Study of Education, Part 1.* Chicago: University of Chicago Press; Richardson, V. (1990). Significant and worthwhile change in teaching practice. *Educational Researcher* 19 (7), 10–18; Richardson, V. (1994). Conducting research on practice. *Educational Researcher* 23 (5), 5–10; Wagner, J. (1997). The unavoidable intervention of educational research: A framework for reconsidering

researcher-practitioner cooperation. *Educational Researcher* 26 (7), 13–22.

5. Jackson, P. W. (1968). *Life in classrooms*. New York: Holt, Rinehart, and Winston; Richardson, V. (1994). Conducting research on practice. *Educational Researcher* 23 (5), 5–10; Shavelson, R. J., and Stern, P. (1981). Research on teachers' pedagogical thoughts, judgments, decisions, and behavior. *Review of Educational Research,* 51, 455–98.

6. See the recommendations presented in NCTM's *Professional standards for teaching mathematics* (Reston, Va.: NCTM, 1991) and those in other recent reform-minded documents, such as Ball, D. L. (1993). With an eye on the mathematical horizon: Dilemmas of teaching elementary school mathematics. *Elementary School Journal* 93, 373–97; Hiebert, J.; Carpenter, T. P.; Fennema, E.; Fuson, K.; Wearne, D.; Murray, H.; Olivier, A.; and Human, P. (1997). *Making sense: Teaching and learning mathematics with understanding.* Portsmouth, N.H.: Heinemann; and Lampert, M. (1985). How do teachers manage to teach? *Harvard Educational Review* 55, 178–94.

7. For reviews of the empirical evidence regarding the effectiveness of this kind of teaching, see Hiebert, J. (1999). Relationships between research and the NCTM Standards. *Journal for Research in Mathematics Education* 30, 3–19; and Hiebert, J.; Carpenter, T. P.; Fennema, E.; Fuson, K.; Wearne, D.; Murray, H.; Olivier, A.; and Human, P. (1997). *Making sense: Teaching and learning mathematics with understanding.* Portsmouth, N.H.: Heinemann. It should be noted that the kind of instruction described in these reports shares many features with the Japanese script for teaching we described in chapters 3 through 6.

8. Ball, D. L. (1993). With an eye on the mathematical horizon: Dilemmas of teaching elementary school mathematics. *Elementary School Journal* 93, 373–97; Ball, D. L. (1996). Teacher learning and the mathematics reforms: What we think we know and what we need to learn. *Phi Delta Kappan* 77, 500–508; Cohen, D. K. (1988). *Teaching practice* (Issue Paper 88-3). East Lansing, Mich.: Michigan State University, National Center for Research on Teacher Education; Lampert, M. (1985). How do teachers manage to teach? *Harvard Educational Review* 55, 178–94; McDonald, J. P. (1992).

Teaching: Making sense of an uncertain craft. New York: Teachers College Press; Schifter, D. (1996). A constructivist perspective on teaching and learning mathematics. *Phi Delta Kappan* 77, 492–99.

CHAPTER 10: THE TRUE PROFESSION
OF TEACHING

1. Feiman-Nemser, S., and Floden, R. (1986). The cultures of teaching. In M. C. Wittrock (ed.), *Handbook of research on teaching.* New York: Macmillan. Pp. 505–26.

2. Apple, M. W. (1986). *Teachers and text.* New York: Routledge and Kegan Paul.

3. See DeVault and Weaver [DeVault, M. V., and Weaver, J. F. (1970). Forces and issues related to curriculum and instruction, K–6. In P. S. Jones (ed.), *A history of mathematics education in the United States and Canada: Thirty-second yearbook.* Washington, D.C.: National Council of Teachers of Mathematics] and Osborne and Crosswhite [Osborne, A. R., and Crosswhite, F. J. (1970). Forces and issues related to curriculum and instruction, 7–12. In Jones, *A history of mathematics education in the United States and Canada*] for a history of the development of mathematics curricula in the United States. An alternative way in which curricula might be developed if we trusted teachers to use them for improving students' learning and for improving their own teaching is presented in Ball, D. L., and Cohen, D. K. (1996). Reform by the book: What is or might be the role of curriculum materials in teacher learning and instructional reform? *Educational Researcher* 25 (9), 6–8, 14.

4. In their 1983 article, L. Darling-Hammond, A. Wise, and S. Pease describe the way in which efforts to analyze the quality of instruction turn into evaluations of teachers by administrators (Teacher evaluation in the organizational context: A review of the literature. *Review of Educational Research* 53, 285–328). The responses of teachers to the kind of distrust signaled by this tendency are described in Griffin, G. A. (1995). Influences of shared decision making on school and classroom activity: Conversations with five teachers. *Elementary School Journal* 96, 29–45; Jackson, P. W. (1968). *Life in classrooms.* New York: Holt, Rinehart, and Winston;

and McDonald, J. P. (1992). *Teaching: Making sense of an uncertain craft.* New York: Teachers College Press.

5. Berliner, D. C., and Biddle, B. J. (1995). *The manufactured crisis: Myths, frauds, and the attack on America's public schools.* New York: Addison Wesley.

6. Carnegie Forum on Education and the Economy. (1986). *A nation prepared: Teachers for the twenty-first century.* Washington, D.C.: Carnegie Forum on Education and the Economy; Holmes Group. (1986). *Tomorrow's teachers: A report of the Holmes Group.* East Lansing, Mich.: Holmes Group; Kerchner, C. T., and Caufman, K. D. (1995). Lurching toward professionalism: The saga of teacher unionism. *Elementary School Journal* 96, 107–22; Romberg, T. A. (1988). Can teachers be professionals? In D. A. Grouws and T. J. Cooney (eds.), *Effective mathematics teaching.* Reston, Va.: National Council of Teachers of Mathematics. Pp. 224–44.

7. Cuban, L. (1993). *How teachers taught: Constancy and change in American classrooms, 1890–1990,* 2nd ed. New York: Teachers College Press; Hoetker, J., and Ahlbrand, W. (1969). The persistence of the recitation. *American Educational Research Journal* 6, 145–67; Tyack, D., and Cuban, L. (1995). *Tinkering toward utopia: A century of public school reform.* Cambridge, Mass.: Harvard University Press.

8. Cohen, D. K., and Hill, H. C. (1998). *Instructional policy and classroom performance: The mathematics reform in California.* Ann Arbor: University of Michigan; Lortie, D. C. (1975). *Schoolteacher: A sociological study.* Chicago: University of Chicago Press; Lubeck, S. (1996). Teachers and the teaching profession in the United States. In *The education system in the United States: Case study findings* (draft volume). Ann Arbor, Mich.: University of Michigan Center for Human Growth and Development. Pp. 241–318; Weiss, I. (1994). *A profile of science and mathematics education in the United States: 1993.* Chapel Hill, N.C.: Horizon Research, Inc.

9. A more complete version of this story can be found in Cremin, L. A. (1964). *The transformation of the school: Progressivism in American education, 1876–1957.* New York: Vintage Books; Johnson, W. R. (1987). Empowering practitioners: Holmes, Carnegie, and lessons of history. *History of Education Quarterly* 27, 221–40; Lagemann, E. C.

(1989). The plural worlds of educational research. *History of Education Research* 29, 185–214; Lagemann, E. C. (1996). Contested terrain: A history of education research in the United States, 1890–1990. *Educational Researcher* 26 (9), 5–17; Tanner, L. N. (1997). *Dewey's laboratory school: Lessons for today.* New York: Teachers College Press; Urban, W. J. (1990). Historical studies of teacher education. In W. R. Houston (ed.), *Handbook of research on teacher education.* New York: Macmillan, pp. 59–71. Other stories of the separation can also be told. See, for example, Linda Darling-Hammond's discussion of other educational figures who contributed to the separation [Darling-Hammond, L. (1997). *The right to learn.* San Francisco: Jossey-Bass].

10. The problem has not gone unnoticed. There are countermovements that try to renegotiate the roles between teacher and researcher, such as the contemporary notion in the research community of "teacher-as-researcher." But none of the countermovements have altered fundamentally the traditional division of labor on a wide scale.

11. The October 1995 testimony is reprinted in the *American Educator* 21 (1, 2), 1997, pp. 35–36.

12. Johnson, W. R. (1996). History and educational reform. *History of Education Quarterly* 36, 478–82.

13. Goldenberg, C. N., and Sullivan, J. (1994). Making change happen in a language-minority school: A search for coherence (EPR #13). Washington, D.C.: Center for Applied Linguistics; Elmore, R. F.; Peterson, P. L.; and McCarthey, S. J. (1996). *Restructuring in the classroom: Teaching, learning, and school organization.* San Francisco: Jossey-Bass; Stein, M. K.; Silver, E. A.; and Smith, M. S. (1998). Mathematics reform and teacher development: A community of practice perspective. In J. Greeno and S. Goldman (eds.), *Thinking practices in mathematics and science learning.* Mahwah, N.J.: Erlbaum.

Index